KB157918

A Study
on Teaching EFL Writing:
Reading-Based Writing Instruction

Min-Joo Kim

국학자료원

ABSTRACT

The purpose of this study was to investigate the effects of reading-based writing instruction that incorporated intertextual and reflective-reading strategies with teacher feedback (IRRF) on the writing performance of Korean undergraduate students enrolled in English for General Purposes (EGP) course.

For 16 weeks, the study examined 102 EFL Korean college students' writing performance across the three following variations of reading-based instruction: no intertextuality, no reflective-reading strategies with teacher feedback (control group); (2) no intertextuality, but reflective-reading strategies with teacher feedback (RRF group);(3) intertextuality, and reflective-reading strategies with teacher feedback (IRRF group). The subjects were in their second year of learning English as a foreign language in college, majoring in fields other than English. The students had their objective and subjective writing performance assessed before and after the study with modified Test of English for International Communication (TOEIC) and Test of English as a Foreign Language (TOEFL) questions. They were also surveyed before and after the study to evaluate their self-awareness and self-confidence in writing.

The control group received traditional instruction, based on comprehension questions (short answers, multiple choice, and true-false statements) through teacher-centered class discussions. The RRF group utilized three reflective-reading x strategies – reading summaries, reading journals, and group discussions – each of which were accompanied by teacher feedbac

k. The IRRF group received the same reflective-reading strategies as the RRF group, with the addition of intertextuality, which was achieved by reading the textbook in intertextual order and providing more backgrou nd information on each reading topic.

In this study, one-way ANCOVAs, one-way ANOVAs, and paired t-test s were used to analyze the data obtained from the pre- and post-tests and surveys. In addition to an examination of the effectiveness of intert extual and reflective-reading strategies with teacher feedback in improvin g overall writing scores, the objective and subjective writing types was also analyzed separately. Five components of writing were also compared before and after the instruction to determine which, if any, was improv ed the most; these five components were content, organization, gramma r, vocabulary, and punctuation. Additionally, the survey results were anal yzed to establish whether the students' self-awareness of their writing pr ocess and their confidence in writing rose over the period of instruction.

The results revealed that the IRRF gained higher scores in the post-exp erimental 'writing test than did the control and RRF groups. IRRF read ing-based writing instruction was also effective in improving both object ive and subjective writing, though its influence on objective writing was greater. IRRF also improved vocabulary and punctuation, while content, organization, and students' self-awareness in writing improved with the application of reflective-reading strategies with teacher feedback on their own with on need for xiadditional intertextuality. Grammar improved in both the RRF and IRRF groups. When considering the IRRF group onl y, content and organization showed greater improvement than grammar, vocabulary, and punctuation. The instruction also raised students' confide nce in writing but this increase was not significant in this study.

The findings provide pedagogical implications for EFL classrooms. The s etting of the study, a single school in Korea with non-English major st udents as the participants, was a major limitation. It is recommended t hat the same instructional model be applied at different educational leve ls and under different conditions in future studies.

Contents

CHAPTER I

INTRODUCTION

1.1 Context of the Study

1.1.1 Foreign Language Learning

The purpose of foreign language learning is to acquire communicative c
ompetence in the target language in order to express knowledge, thoug
hts, emotions, and feelings in that language (Brown, 1994). Communica
tive competence refers to the ability of learners to convey and interpret
messages as well as negotiate meaning within specificcontexts. Therefore,
it depends on both the cooperation of the participants involved anddyna
mic and interpersonal construction which can only be determined by ex
amining the overt performance of two or more individuals, in the proce
ss of communication (Day & Bamford, 1998). According to Lee and Pa
ttern (1995), communicative competence in language learning is assume
d to consist of two mains aspects: organization and pragmatism. The fo
rmer is a combination of grammatical and textual competence including
mastery of vocabulary, morphology, syntax, phonology, text cohesion, an
d rhetorical organization. In contrast, the latter is a combination of illoc
utionary and sociolinguistic competence, including ideational and manipu
lative competence, imaginative functions, sensitivity to dialect, cultural re

ferences, and figures of speech. Competency in both organization and pr agmatism, more commonly referred to as form and content, respectively is expected for successful communication.

In order to ensure understandable communication with others, foreign la nguage education focuses on the four language skills: reading and listeni ng (receptive skills), and speaking and writing (productive skills; Brown, 2007). Though these four skills should ideally have equal weight in En glish as a Foreign Language (EFL) learning, the reality is that many cla ssrooms still follow a traditional method of instruction based on reading and grammar (Murray, 2008). Indeed, influenced by the oldest method of language instruction, grammar-translation, EFL education has long be en dominated by the linguistic and syntactical point of view, which enc ourages the breaking down of text into its individual components (e.g., paragraphs, sentences, words) in order to understand meaning (Nabei & Swain, 2002). For this reason, reading is often the first skill introduced in language classrooms. Though a vital skill in genuine communication, an overemphasis on reading can leave students with undeveloped speaki ng and listening skills.

Thus, despite a mastery of reading and listening, it is not uncommon f or language learners to be unable to produce communicatively competen t language orally or in writing. As suggested by Kimura (2001), if a le arner cannot produce appropriate feedback in conversation, genuine com munication cannot be said to be taking place and as such foreign langu age learning is more effective when the four skills are acquired togethe r. Thus, in order for learners to acquire more balanced communicative c ompetence, a recent trend in foreign language education and communica tive teaching and learning has been a shift of focus from receptive to p roductive skills (Agazade &Vefali, 2013). Of the two productive skills, h owever, more emphasis has been placed on the development of speaking than it has on writing (Holliday, 1994). Indeed, the field of foreign lan guage education has privileged spoken language as the primary modality of production (Carson, 2001).

However, as highlighted by Drucker (2003) and Watts-Taffe and Trusc ott (2000), oral language competency is only one element of language proficiency and it alone cannot explain the language ability of a learner as a whole. This biased attention to the development of speaking skills has resulted in the stagnation of writing skills in many learners. In this context, Larsen-Freeman (1991) and Skehan (1998) observed that equal importance and attention should be ascribed to written language for eff ective and balanced communication. According to these researchers, learn ing and communicating in a foreign language requires a through and e qually proficient development of reading, listening, speaking, and writin g. Therefore, the teaching and learning of both oral and written langua ge should occur simultaneously.

1.1.2 Importance and Benefits of Teaching English Writing

Writing is an important part of communication and is highly valued as a mode of general learning (Grabe, 2001). As suggested by Gutierrez (1992) and Harklau (2002), writing as a tool of instruction is an especi ally effective method for foreign language acquisition. For example, the learning and use of common phrases and grammatical rules can be foste red through writing (Carson & Leki, 1993). Writing also helps learners to express their current level of language proficiency without requiring direct comparison with others' (Peregoy & Boyle, 1991).

In addition to boosting language development in general, writing also p ositively affects reading performance and vocabulary learning (Valdes, 19 99). While writing, grammatical forms and syntactic structures can be practiced and mastered by learners (Matsuda & De Pew, 2002). This ab ility can be transferred to the reading experience and assists reading dev elopment, as reading involves similar processes, such as discovering the meaning of words, analyzing syntactic structures, and interpreting gram matical forms (Lenski & Johns, 2000). Moreover, writing also benefits le xical knowledge because vocabulary brainstorming and mind maps, whic h can be done in the prewriting stage, encourage learners to consider a nd subsequently use more sophisticated words (Muncie, 2002). In additi on, through contextual writing, the active processing of defining words serves to foster vocabulary development (Tribble, 1996).

Furthermore, writing can help develop critical and cognitive thinking. A ccording to Quitadamo and Kurtz (2007), critical thinking is an "intent ional, self-regulated process that provides a mechanism for solving probl ems and making decisions based on reasoning and logic" (p. 141). They reported that laboratory writing in biology education increases critical th inking, along with analysis, inference, and evaluation skills. The study c oncluded that writing has a positive influence on students' critical thinki ng performance. In an examination of the effects of writing on the criti cal thinking process, Langer and Applebee (1987) argued that classroom activities involving writing lead to better learning compared to activities using only reading and studying. They also observed that different types of writing activities at secondary school promoted a variety of thinking skills; while analytic writing was found to be beneficial for deeper reaso ning and text selection, summary writing and note-taking promoted effe ctive comprehension.

1.1.3 Approaches in Teaching Writing

Given the importance of providing targeted English writing education, e fforts to improve learner writing skills has led to the emergence and de velopment of two representative approaches to the teaching of writing: conventional and unconventional (Atkinson, 2008). According to Atkinso n (2008), the conventional approach focuses on practicing certain format s and expressions with imitation and repetition, including grammar trans lation, the direct method, and the audio-lingual, cognitive, and situation al reinforcement approaches. The unconventional approach, on the other hand, focuses on fostering the creative expression of a learner's opinion i n a natural communicative setting and includes such methods as the sil ent way, community language learning, suggestopedia, and total physical response. As Atkinson (2008) and Grabe and Kaplan (1996) suggested, the difference between the two approaches is the way in which languag e learners reach their outcomes. Whereas students are expected to write in certain ways in conventional teaching, they are expected to come up with their own ideas in unconventional settings (Atkinson, 2008; Grabe & Kaplan, 1996; Hyland, 2003). Thus, the former is a teacher-centered approach, while the latter is learner-focused. The unconventional approac h has been considered the more effective method of teaching writing (L arsen-Freeman, 1998). Through the promotion of the writing process its elf, students often feel more at ease with composition and are able to e xplore their writing skills, rather than simply adhering to the teacher in structions (Simon, 2011).

As the unconventional approach was assumed by many scholars to be a more appropriate way of teaching and learning English writing, the role of the writer in the EFL language classroom changed (McCarthey,

Guo, & Cummins, 2005). Previously, students produced what the teac
her asked under specific direction, but the more recent method of teac
hing writing acknowledges the students as creative writers capable of c
reating multiple meanings through written language. Therefore, the un
conventional teaching approach has urged teachers to consider their rea
ders' identity, background knowledge, and expectations (Brown, 2007;
Carson, Carrell, Silberstein, Kroll, & Kuehn, 1990; Valdes, 1999). Thu
s, learners should be allowed to vary the content, organization, and li
nguistic expression of their writing depending on their understanding o
f the potential audience. This way of thinking provides writers with a
uthority, and successful communication with the reader thus depends o
n the writers themselves. With this new-found authority, students as
writers are able to package their thoughts as cohesive units privileging
content over form.

1.1.4 Problems in Teaching EFL Writing in College

Although this new approach to EFL writing education has the support
of a number of researchers operating from a theoretical perspective, man
y practical problems currently remain in writing classrooms at college.
Most universities around the world offer English writing programs as re
quired courses for graduation, treating them as English for general purp
ose (EGP) courses (Celce-Murcia & McIntosh, 1991). However, according
to Hyland (2003) and Truscott (1999), these programs face many limita
tions that impede students from improving their writing.

Of the numerous problems encountered in EFL writing education, the
most serious is an outdated pedagogical approach to the subject (Arche

r, 2001). Although the concept of writing in EFL has shifted from the mere reproduction of a teacher's requirements for a class assignment to wards expressing a learner's own opinion as a means of communication, neither the overall understanding of writing education, nor the style of teaching has changed. Based on the old-fashioned perspective on learnin g writing, students are still found to be practicing grammar-oriented, se ntence-level, and translation-focused writing in class.

Another common problem in EFL writing education is the use of teach er- centered methodologies (Weigle, 2002). As indicated by Simin and Tavangar (2009), the teacher's role should be to encourage students to write and revise their own writing rather than to point out every lingui stic form that is not used appropriately. Al-Hazmi and Schofield (2007) and Swales (1990) also argued that, while student-led revision without direct assistance from the teacher would inevitably take more time, cont inuous self-correction of content and writing style would eventually have stronger long-term effects. However, in many current writing classes, te achers tend to provide direct feedback on their students' writing, taking away the opportunity for students' self-development (Marefat, 2007). If this correction strategy remains commonplace, students will continue to struggle to acquire self-correction skills in writing (Hyland, 2002).

The short comings of the teacher-centered approaches to writing instruct ion are also intrinsically linked to the lack of high quality EFL writing education for non-native English speaker (NNES) teachers (Hyland, 200 2). According to Knapp and Watkins (1994), Ping and Wenjie (2001) and Hyland (2002), in current EFL writing education, most teachers are NNESs who have rarely received writing instruction in an English-speak ing country. Therefore, their own EFL writing instruction tends to rely on the teaching methods they are familiar with in their first language. L eki (2001) also highlighted the lack of experience in English writing and teaching for NNES teachers, which leads to instructional problems in the classrooms. Thus, NNES teachers are unaware of the most effective strat egies available to teach writing in an EFL setting. Even some native En glish speaker (NES) teachers have not developed the requisite proficiency in English writing, which means that they are not particularly qualified to teach it (Weigle, 2002). Many of the teachers in this situation major ed in a subject other than English or English education, and have merel y obtained short-term certification to teach English in Korea. This lack of effective teacher training for both NNES and NES teachers of English decreases the chance of raising students' writing ability (Swales, 1990).

In addition to unprepared and unqualified writing teachers, an instructional problem is also endemic in EFL Korean classroom settings (Choi & Seong, 2011). Many colleges in Korea have started to offer English composition courses as an English for General Purposes (EGP) program. However, there are many limitations and problems in English writing classes in Korean colleges that are similar to those in EFL writing programs outside of Korea, including the use of grammar- and translation-oriented methods, teacher-centered error correction, and systematic educational problems. Above all, the most frequently used but most problematic method in Korean EFL writing classes is explicit grammar instruction (Hwang, 2013). For example, students may be given a printed handout of Korean sentences and then requested to translate these sentences into English. However, this practice of focusing on single sentences can encourage students to approach writing as a string of isolated ideas rather than a coherent unit consisting of a theme and supporting idea. While this sentence-level practice helps students to write grammatically correct sentences, it does little to help them outline and write paragraphs and essays. In addition, without a focus on transitional words and linking phrases, the English writing of

Korean students tend to simply reflect the translation of their thoughts in Korean, with the help of an English dictionary. Rewriting sentences in another language is not true writing; it is just translation practice (Barnes & Lock, 2010).

A number of writing classes are taught by Korean instructors who simpl y correct student mistakes and awkward expressions (Lee & Oxford, 200 8). According to Park(2013), Korean teachers of English focus on error c orrection, which does not promote the cognitive processes necessary to ge nerate ideas through the written word. Students are provided with direct feedback on incorrect language use, rather than indirect feedback, such as the underlining of non-standard expressions, so that they can revise and r ewrite them. Similarly, Choi (2008) argued that if a teacher lowers grade s for spelling or other systematic errors, students' learning stress increases, which eventually creates a psychological barrier to learning. In addition t o this, while students may come to learn correct spelling and phrases, in vesting their energy in word memorization can lead to a failure to constr uct accurate sentences and manage the content of a composition.

If the present learning conditions remain unchanged, the continuous me morization of new vocabulary, phrases, and grammatical rules may event ually result in many students losing interest in English writing. Therefo re, error correction in EFL instruction should be provided in the form o f indirect questions or guidelines rather than direct comments that elimi nate the possibility of student self-correction.

Alongside the instructional problems mentioned above, English writing e ducation has not been properly conducted in Korea (Pae, 2012). In con trast to reading, listening, and speaking, writing has largely been neglec ted. Although students are required to study English as a school subject from elementary to high school, the purpose of their study is to pass t he college entrance exam, not to develop writing skills. Therefore, Kore an students have rarely been exposed to effective writing education, and thus do not recognize the importance of writing until they enroll in E GP courses after entering college. Only after being assigned their first f ormal composition in English do they recognize the need for writing ab ility (Cho, 2012). Therefore, most Korean college students are novices i n English writing and thus lack confidence. For these students, the curr ent methods of English writing instruction have not proven effective, an d there is urgent need for a change.

1.1.5 Problems in Reading-Based Writing Model

Reading-based writing instruction helps students internalize reading mate rials and connect them to writing (Grabe, 2003). In this process, stude nts can apply the content of the reading to their previous knowledge b y drawing on their own experiences. They can then put these experienc es into writing as a means of expressing their feelings, empathy, though ts, and future plans. With reading-based writing instruction, students ar e able to communicate with others by escaping from sentence-level com position, and focusing on the bigger picture (Yeh, 2001). Reading-based writing is also more helpful than grammar practice and repetition-style writing practice (Rao, 2005).

Although reading-based writing is beneficial, in that it results in a bett er understanding of the reading materials and the transferability of readi ng to writing skills in EFL classrooms, problems with this type of instr uction have nevertheless been observed. The first limitation relates to th e instructional approach, specifically, how to connect the knowledge lear ned from the reading to the writing (Ferris & Roberts, 2001). How tea chers explain the internalization process of reading, transforming the ma terial into knowledge the students can absorb, and then subsequently ac cessing that knowledge and putting it into writing, has been a crucial issue in reading-based writing research in EFL learning. The most commonly used method at present is selecting sentence patterns from texts, and letting students practice writing based on those patterns. Using the same structure, students change elements of the sentence, such as the subject, verb, or context, and create a new sentence. However, students do not develop beyond this level; they tend to use the same pattern and style over and over in their writing.

Added to this, in most classes, it is often the teacher who selects the useful expressions from the reading (De Larios, Murphy, & Manchon, 1999). The most negative aspect of this instructional approach is that it lowers student autonomy. Students should practice choosing phrases and vocabulary from readings on their own, considering which ones are the most important and useful for writing. The teacher's job is to provide students with strategies to improve their writing and develop their learning skills even after completing the college course. The previous approach to reading-based writing instruction does not promote self-directed learning or the concept of a lifelong learner.

Most Korean college students have little chance to continue studying English writing outside of their EGP composition course (Choi, 2010). Apart from English majors who may practice writing in English in some of their major classes, most other students only learn English writing in EGP classes. Therefore, most Korean EFL college students are unable to develop their writing skills beyond the expressions their writing teachers chose for them.

Another limitation of reading-based writing instruction lies in the lack of intertextuality in reading materials. Intertextuality is defined as background knowledge of the reading materials and the presented order of texts (Beach, Boyd & Maloof, 2000). The comprehension of a set of texts is aided by reading them in logical order, allowing learners' to revise th eir previous knowledge and acquire new information.Therefore, it is ben eficial for both the critical reading of a particular text and the cognitiv e development of students. Building intertextual connections, developing a more meaningful interaction between the reader and the text, and ob taining linguistic ability in the target language help learners to improve not only their reading comprehension but also their reading skills. Despi te these advantages, however, previous reading-based writing research co nducted in an EFL setting has tended not to consider intertextuality an important issue.

1.1.6 New Model: Reading-Based Writing with Reflective-Re ading Strategies

Intertextuality in reading has a positive effect on students' understandin g of reading materials; however, taken alone, it cannot ensure internaliz ation of the content into students' existing knowledge and a smooth tra nsition to writing output. Reflective reading strategies can therefore be a powerful addition to the reading-based writing to reinforce the process as a whole (Alger, 2006). Teaching reflective reading has proven to be an effective learning tool because it leads to a more through comprehen sion of reading content, more efficient internalization, and a more fluent production of writing.

Much like with intertextual-reading, reflective-reading helps to develop b etter comprehension of reading materials (Warin, Maddock, Pell, & Har greaves, 2006). This strategy asks questions about previous experiences helping to conceptualize the reader's state of mind and on-going behavi ors. It also develops a constant and critical look at the learning process.

With reflective reading, readers can connect their better understanding o
f the text to their own knowledge by reminding themselves of and revi
ewing previous academic and personal experiences. Yinger (1990) argued
that the reflective-reading strategy involves solving problems as well as
the active, persistent, and careful consideration of knowledge.

Along with self-directed learning, self-analysis, and self-evaluation skills,
reflective learning also promotes open-mindedness, responsibility, and wh
oleheartedness (Alger, 2006). It is also known to promote the internaliz
ation of reading content. It is an active, performative, and conscious lea
rning process. By looking back at past events, learners can be more crit
ical and evaluative, and through repetition, they can create new informa
tion. The production of coherent pieces of writing based on reading is
aided by this process. Furthermore, differentiated characterized learning i
s possible with the use of reflective strategies; students can exhibit diffe
rent writing outcomes from the same reading material. As Day (1993)
reported, a reflective-reading strategy is also productive; examining what
happened previously, learners can develop a broader perspective. In addi
tion, according to Sue and Harrison (2008), reflective learning practice
helps improve observation, communication, judgment, decision-making, a
nd team-work. Their study of teacher training using a reflective-reading
strategy has also found that it is more effective for beginning-level than
higher level learners.

According to previous research on reflective-reading strategies in reading-
based writing, there is also a need for quality teacher feedback on stud
ents' reflection (Dewar, Servos, Bosacki, & Coplan, 2013). In this contex
t, teacher feedback is expected not only to enhance reading comprehensi
on, the internalization of content, and the connection to personal knowl
edge and experience, but also to improve writing results. support of th
e positive effect of teacher feedback, Hyland (2003) argued that it incre

ases the quality of learning by considering students' individual difference s. acher feedback is also known to boost students' motivation and self-c onfidence (Nation, 2009).

However, in EFL learning, especially at the elementary and low-interme diate levels, students tend to obediently follow the feedback of the teac her in other words; the teacher is idolized (Ferris, 2003). Students are t herefore unable to develop their own opinions, and instead a passive att itude to learning is unintentionally reinforced.

Therefore, teacher feedback is better if it is indirect and asks questions rather than providing explicit comments or direct instruction. With teac her feedback on students' reading-reflection, students can better understa nd the nature of reading-based writing and the reasons for using readin g materials as writing input and thus will eventually be expected to pr oduce better quality writing.

1.1.7 The Significance of the Current Study

Regarding aforementioned problems and limitations in EFL writing educ ation in Korea, the present study aims to present a new instructional model for EFL writing and investigate its effects. This model is based o n the integration of intertextual reading-based writing instruction with r eflective components and appropriate teacher feedback.

The combination of these two factors, intertextuality and reflective-readi ng strategies with teacher feedback reading-based writing will help to s olve previously established problems with reading-based EFL writing. Th e proposed model can provide a natural setting rather than artificial set ting for the reading and help develop self-studying skills.The indirect g uidance that will be part of the teacher feedback will help students foc us more on content than form. This instructional model is expected to positively affect students' writing development by promoting a learner-centered, self-motivated, and self-directed learning approach in EFL writing. It is also expected to support the practice of genuine self-expression in composition, where students can brainstorm their own ideas without a teacher's intervention. The combination of the two factors, intertextuality and reflective-reading strategies with teacher feedback, thus aimed to solve the previously reported problems in reading-based writing instruction in the EFL environment.

The proposed model is based on the following assumptions: 1) intertextual and reflective-reading strategies with teacher feedback (IRRF) in reading-based writing instruction has an impact on writing performance in college EFL writing classrooms, 2) IRRF reading-based writing instruction has an impact on both objective and subjective types of writing, 3) IRRF reading-based writing instruction has an impact on various components of writing, including content, organization, grammar, vocabulary, and spelling. 4) IRRF reading-based writing instruction has an impact on students' self-awareness regarding their writing, and 5) IRRF reading-based writing instruction has an impact on students' self-confidence in their writing.

1.2 Purpose of the Study

The present study aims to find an effective reading-based writing instruction that will help Korean EFL college students enrolled in EGP courses to improve their composition skills. As previously mentioned, reading-based writing instruction has been reported to achieve positive outcomes in writing performance in an EFL environment. The present study thus introduced intertextual and reflective-reading strategies with teacher feed back (IRRF) reading-based writing instruction to Korean EFL college stu dents in EGP classes. It is assumed that IRRF will be an effective tool for enhancing EFL students' understanding of the reading materials used in class, for improving self-studying skills, and eventually for developing their writing ability. *Writing development* in this study refers to the i mprovement in writing performance by participating students in the fo llowing five categories: content, organization, grammar, vocabulary, and punctuation. A detailed description of each of these components is pro vided in Chapter III.

The findings provide an effective reading-based writing instructional mod el that can solve problems associated with traditional EFL writing instru ction. The results also have practical implications for college EGP writin g classes in the sense that IRRF reading-based writing instruction enhan ces students' writing ability. Intertextuality (I), which focuses on the bac kground schema of reading content and the relationship between texts, reflective-reading strategies (RR), which focus on the relationship betwee n texts and learners, and teacher feedback (F), which focuses on the rel ationship between learners and teachers, together increase the strength t he relationship between the reading texts, learners, and teachers.

1.3 Research Questions

The purpose of the present study was to examine the effects of intertex tual and reflective-reading strategies (IRRF) reading-based writing instruc tion on Korean EFL students' writing development, as measured by writ ing performance, writing self-awareness of writing, and self-confidence in English writing.

The following five research questions were addressed in the current study:

1. What effect does IRRF reading-based writing instruction have on students' EFL writing performance?

2. Which type of writing is affected most by IRRF reading-based writing instruction?

3. Which component of writing is most effectively improved by IRRF reading-based writing instruction?

4. What effect does IRRF reading-based writing instruction have on students' self-awareness regarding English writing?

5. What effect does IRRF reading-based writing instruction have on the students' self-confidence in English writing?

CHAPTER II

REVIEW OF LITERATURE

This chapter will present the theoretical background of the study, starti ng with the importance of EFL writing education. The following four fa ctors will then be discussed:a) reading-based writing, b) intertextuality i n reading, c) reflective-reading strategies, and d) teacher feedback. Follo wing this, the theoretical background to objective and subjective writin g, two main forms of writing evaluated in this study, will be also prese nted along with self-awareness and self-confidence in EFL learning.

2.1 Changes in EFL Writing Education

In recent years, educators and researchers have started to focus on the equal development of all language skills, rather than on a single area s uch as listening or reading (Haklau, 2002; Lee & Schallert, 2008). This new integrative approach also encouraged a new understanding of writte n language. Grabe (2001) argued that writing is one of the most impo rtant methods of communication between users of English. However, wr iting is not a simple combination of letters; rather, it involves the const ruction of cohesive and meaningful sentences (Ferris & Hedgcock, 1998; Lenski & Johns, 2000). Therefore, effective writing requires conscious eff ort and specialized education. In EFL, learners of English also face the l anguage barrier in the process of improving their L2 writing. As a resu lt, they have to be simultaneously trained in the composition of written language and the natural way to express their ideas in English. In disc ussing the meaning of writing in English education, Atkinson (2008) cla imed that writing is a communicative process and a writer should thus needs to consider the prospective audience in terms of who will read it, what their reading background is and what they expect from the writin g. Therefore, the path to successful writing requires a stage where the l earners organize their thoughts and writing education needs to address t his requirement.

As the importance of teaching writing has gained attention from scholar s, methods of writing instruction have come under investigation as well. In particular, there has been a move towards teaching strategies that e mphasize the meaning of sentences rather than accurate structure and fo rm. In view of this change of focus, learners require education and inst ruction specifically designed to encourage improvement in their written communication, especially in an EFL setting. Grammatically correct sent ences, appropriate vocabulary choices, effective writing style, and the log ical communication of one's thoughts all need to be learnt (Tribble,Thes e linguistic issues in EFL composition consume much of a learner's time and should be taught when the native language and English have differ ent linguistic backgrounds.

Another major improvement in EFL writing education can occur when c ultural differences in thinking patterns in written composition are taken into account (Grabe & Kaplan, 1998; Hyland, 2002). For example, Celc e-Murcia and McIntosh (1991), and Truscott (1999) suggested that stud ents whose L1 is English tend to write short introductions in order to attract their readers' attention and write clear, direct sentences to clearl y convey meaning and purpose. In comparison, students' learning EFL t end to write longer introductions and do not clearly and succinctly artic ulate their purpose for writing. In addition, while their lexical and gra mmatical repertoire will expand and become more sophisticated after lea rning the syntactic and semantic structures of English, EFL students are often still unfamiliar with the native way of writing in English, and so cannot achieve cohesive compositions.

In summary, EFL writing education has three clear instruction goals: te aching a cohesive style of writing, encouraging English-style logical thin king, and overcoming the language barrier. Since students find it difficu lt to improve all three of these areas by themselves, more effective met hods of teaching writing are needed in order to improve EFL learners' writing performance.

2.2 Current Theories about EFL Writing Education

In the current EFL writing classroom, two major theories underpin the most commonly used instructional strategies: direct models and indirect models of reading for writing (Hirvela, 2004). The direct model include s mining, writerly reading, rhetorical reading, and the modeling approac h. According to Greene (1992), indirect mining is similar to the critical reading of text where readers consider the reading content as a valuable source for writing. The author shows that readers can learn "rhetorical, linguistic, [and] lexical input" (p. 36) through mining reading materials. This notion is similar to writerly reading, which views reading as a pre-stage for writing (Iida, 2008). Along similar lines, Hunt (1985) claimed that readers often read texts as if they were writing them. Carrell (199 1) supported this notion by stating that rhetorical reading analyzes the reading content and applies notable features to subsequent writing. The modeling approach focuses on practicing close reading and using similar styles and structures in subsequent writing (Barkaoui, 2007). Smagorinsky (1992) further explained that writing students internalize the format and correctness of a text while reading and these aspects become a template for the composition.

The indirect model is characterized by extensive reading and voluntary reading. Extensive reading is based on the assumption that simply reading a large number of diverse sources allows students to naturally acquire a linguistically and culturally appropriate form of writing. In his examination of extensive reading in South Pacific and Southeast Asian schools, Elley (1991) noted its effectiveness in writing development. Voluntary reading, on the other hand, allows for students' own choice of reading list and expects personal motivation and the joy of reading in itself to become a useful basis for writing. Kim and Krashen (1997) pointed out that "free voluntary reading is a powerful means of developing second language competence" (p. 26). The authors also observe that voluntary reading helps to improve grammar, spelling, and composition skills.

In addition to these two theories, there are currently two broad types of writing instruction widely used in EFL classrooms. One is the teaching of writing itself(Connor, 1996; Manchón, 2009). This type of class practices different genres of writing, such as narrative, opinion, descriptive, and process. Students are asked to compose essays based on assigned topics, which are then handed in for the teacher's comments. Grammar instruction usually accompanies this process. The other type of writing instruction is based on reading (Shokrpour & Fallahzadeh, 2007). This type of class provides as much reading materials as possible during class and expects the students to naturally acquire composition skills with the teacher guiding the students towards making connections between the r eading and writing. This form of reading-based writing instruction comp lements the view that writing education should respect and recognize th e individual character of each student and pursue the cohesion and cohe rence in a composition rather than formal and technical mastery (Simps on, 2006).

Investigating EFL writing classes taught these two ways, Xiangyun (200 7) observed that the second type of writing instruction was more effecti ve than the first at improving the quality of student compositions. His findings emphasized that teaching writing independently of reading is a deductive process that focuses on delivering set common phrases and se ntence patterns to the students, while reading-based writing instruction asks students to independently identify useful sentence patterns and writ ing structure. As a result, reading-based writing instruction leads to mo re native like compositions, highlighting the importance of teaching writ ing through reading.

2.3 Reading to Improve Writing

2.3.1 The Interconnectedness of Reading and Writing

Reading and writing were considered separate skills in learning until the 1970s, with reading a receptive and writing a productive skill. During the 1970s and 1980s, interest in the writing process started to develop, raising questions about the relationship between writing and reading (H are, 1992). By the 100-s, reading and writing were both considered int erpersonal and sociolinguistic functions and this was reflected in the rese arch of this period. For example, scholars such as Eckoff (1993) and Ti erney and Shanahan (1997) claiming that reading and writing shared si milar meta, content, general text, and procedural knowledge bases. Grav e (2003) and Esmaeili (2002) also argues that reading and writing affec ted each other and worked together in learning. Therefore, many resear chers assert that it is better to teach and acquire these two skills toget her rather than separately.

Many studies examining the positive relationship between reading and w riting in a native language (L1) can be categorized into the following t hree groups: reading to writing, writing to reading, and reading and wr iting for learning in general (Greene, 1992; Kroll, 1993; Leki, 1993). I n the L1 context, reading is considered to be a crucial input for writin g (Carson et al., 1990). Boughey (1997) asserted that students can lear n from reading such elements of writing as register, genre, and spellin g. The positive relationship between reading and writing is also evident across different levels of proficiency. According to Crowhurst (1991) and Flahive and Bailey (1993), students' reading levels influenced their writi ng for both fluent and less fluent readers. Fluent readers tended to be better at panning for writing, especially in the period from after-reading to pre-writing. They also wrote more extensively and were better at org anization and producing content. Moreover, the cohesive nature of their writing resulted in higher scores than the corresponding output of less f luent readers.

Most recent studies on the integration of reading and writing in L1 ha ve focused on content and developing critical literary skills. Again, most researchers recommended teaching the two together. In a study by Har e (1992), struggling learners were found to perform better when they s tudied both reading and writing together, and Greene (1993) claimed t hat connecting reading and writing facilitates students' understanding of other subjects, such as history, science, and social science. This strategy has also been to increase students' critical literacy and range of perspect ives on target subjects and can also lead to a faster acquisition of litera

ry in itself. Furthermore, learning the two skills together fulfills more s
pecific needs such as writing business emails, asking a friend for help, a
nd writing to professors (Tierney & Shanahan, 1996).

Students studying English as a second language can also learn how to t
ransfer the knowledge acquired from reading to writing and vice versa
while dealing with those individual needs at the same time. Hirvela (20
04) found support for this idea in his own experience, asserting that bo
th skills share similar processes. As a teacher of both native and non-na
tive speakers of English for reading and writing, he tried teaching readi
ng and writing both separately and together. In his classroom experienc
e, teaching both together enhances students' ability to compose writing
in English especially for non-native speakers: "Since that time, I have b
een convinced that, like many other L2 writing teachers, one of the bes
t ways to improve writing is to improve reading" (pp. 10-11). Hence, i
n order to be fully understood and appreciated, reading and writing sho
uld be viewed, learned, and used together for combined instruction; thu
s, reading to write can lead to improvements in writing.

Klerman (2013), Mulcahy-Ernt & Stewart (1994), and Vygotsky (2012)
have indicated that while interacting with a text, readers communicated
with the author and become writers themselves since their own commu
nication stem from what they have understood until that point. As the
authors explain, new ideas learned from reading become innner thoughts
and thus many reappear later in writing; thus, reading is a form of soc
ial interaction. Zhixue Shaoshan (2003) also found clear evidence of a p
rositive relationship between reading and writing in the transfer of com
munication. They found that chlidren who writer at a level superior to
their peers and at an upper-intermediate level also read above their rea
dinage. Studnets studying reading and writing together learn to underst
and the social and communicative nature of literacy. El-Hindi (2003, p.

359) demonstrated the interactional relationship of reading and writing i
n his study of th emetacognitive connection between the two (figure 1).

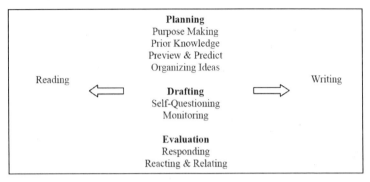

Figure 1 Metacognitive Connection of Reading and Writing
(El-Hindi, 2003, p.359)

Reading and writing as forms of social interaction share similar strategie
s and are both acts of composing. They commonly need the following i
nteraction strategies: goal-setting, knowledge mobilization, projection, per
spective-taking, refinement, review, self-correction, self-assessment, report,
reproduction, paraphrase, predicting outcomes, inference, imagination, mo
nitoring, and creating scenarios (Peng & Yuwen, 2003). In addition, me
aning-making strategies such as monitoring, phrase content, using prior
content knowledge, using text from knowledge, rereading, questioning, a
nd making connections to the author and audience have been shown to
be common in both reading and writing (Yan, 2004).

In Li's (2005) study using storybooks, students used the same strategies
they used in reading and writing. In the production of a piece of writi
ng, which they learned from reading structure, the supportive relationshi
p between the two emerged. In another study teaching writing with co
mic books, Johns (2005) found that students'reading affects their writin
g because they use similar learning strategies. As a result, most features
of comic books were well-represented in their writing.

In addition to the strategies they have in common, reading and writing skills are also similar because learning transfer occur freely between them. Futhermore, reading and writing are complementary, which means that growth in one leads to growth in the other (Rifkin, 2013). Acknowledgement of vocabulary and orthography, which are crucial in understanding text, is essential to the development of writing. A study by Susser (1994) highlighted that a stronger knowledge of vocabulary in reading results in more proficient spelling in writing. Thus, reading and writing are both maximized when viewed as interactive; in fact, word recognition, spelling, reading comprehension, writing quality, lexical and phonemic structure, organizational-structural information, selected comprehension scores, writing measures, the use of cohesive ties, and cohesive harmony in writing has a strong relationship with reading comprehension performance.

In the transferal process of these learning strategies and skills in reading-writing, three directional perspectives can be discerned (Grabe, 2004). The first is the unidirectional model, either from reading to writing, or writing to reading. Generally speaking, most strategies and skills from one skill are easily transferrable to the other. However, the influence of reading on writing is more pronounced than the opposite. Previous studies have proven that the writing to reading direction requires additional writing instruction. The second is a nondirectional model. It claims that reading and writing come from a single underlying proficiency because both are constructive processes and require similar competences. The third is a bidirectional model. It argues that reading and writing are simultaneously independent and interactive. Just like the first model, reading to writing has a higher rate of knowledge transfer than writing to reading.

Numerous studies have reported the advantages of reading-based writin g instruction. For example, Caudery's (1998) study reported that stude nts with free reading classes show great improvement in writing comp ared to those who receive traditional instruction. Therefore, Caudery (1 998) concluded that reading alone is as effective as formal instruction for spelling and vocabulary development. Using the lexical, syntactic, a nd textural features of the readings they are exposed to, students can produce writing content. Likewise, Nam (2008) asserted that reading a variety of content can help students know what and how to write. Ede and Lunsford (1990) also argued that reading is a potent source of new ideas that can be used in writing. The authors introduce the following correlations between reading and writing (p. 125):

1. Better writers tend to be better readers.

2. Better writers read more than poorer writers.

3. Better readers tend to produce more syntactically mature writing tha n poorer readers.

Therefore, Ede and Lunsford (1990) assumed that, as students read mor e, they will write better because what they write comes from what the y read. Students' understanding of previous reading materials is believed to be the most salient factor that influencing the development of writin g skills.

In Pope's (2006) study, where students were asked to read certain types of poetry and then to write similar content, reading was shown to prov ide material for writing, which indicates that reading and writing are in terrelated. Negrettie and Kuteeva's (2011) and Reid's (1996) studies also

demonstrated that connected activities enhance students' higher-order thi
nking. Improvement in content, organization, and language use was also
reported in Schnack (2001) and according to Jinlin, Zhong, and Shuzhe
n (2013), reading to write also generated more interest in the topic. Fu
rther, Hayes (1996) argues that writing involves the following three ste
ps: text interpretation, reflection, and text production. During the writin
g process, the writer continuously produces text, understands it, and re
writes it, all of which are intrinsically related to the activity of reading.
Hayes *1996) also mentioned that in order to produce and write text,
writing should call on knowledge from both long-term and short-term
memory. This knowledge is based on what the writer has preciously rea
d; therefore, what has been read becomes what is written (Fitzgerald &
Shanahan, 2000).

Other studies have also established that reading-based writing is greatly
beneficial in other areas. Swanson and Berninger (1996) reported that st
udents' knowledge acquisition, skill development, thinking ability, and k
nowledge transformation is possible within reading-based writing. Bough
ey's (1997) study found that student's acquisition of knowledge improve
s with reading-based writing instruction while Flahive and Bailey (1993)
attested that reading and writing skills and thinking ability develop and
improve under reading-based writing instruction. Greene (1992) also clai
med that the cognitive engagement of students is extended and enriche
d in reading-based writing. The activity of connecting reading to writin
g asks students to analyze reading content, summarize it, and find a re
lationship to the writing topic. Students also have to brainstorm in orde
r to determine what content is relevant and to develop a coherent writi
ng structure. During the process of reading-based writing, students' cog
nitive and analytic skills are also expected to improve (Greene, 1992). I
n addition, studying writing in the context of reading promotes learner

s' active involvement, and encourages them to think about the writing topic (Yang, 2012). The information that learners gain from reading is communicated to others through writing. Reading puts a learner in the position of a listener and receiver of knowledge, whereas writing positions them as a speaker and provider. Thus, both writing-before-reading and writing-after-reading have positive effects on learning; while writing-before-reading helps readers better understand the text as well as infer character traits, writing-after-reading helps readers review the meaning they derived from the text (De Ryker & Ponnudurai, 2011).

2.3.2 Teaching Reading-Based Writing

English reading education that considers the intimate relationship between reading and writing positively influences writing skills. A teacher who helps students connect the two should act as a guide to promote thinking and understanding; in other words, learning should be a learner-centered process (Crowhurst, Yang, Badger, & Yu, 2006). In the long term, integrated learning reading and writing enables the acquisition of critical literacy as shown in Mungtaisong's (2003) study on workshop organization. This integration has also been found to be beneficial for theme development, diverse literary selection, and strategy planning. Developing the two skills together also promotes self-directed strategic learning that can be called upon after students finish their former education. As mentioned above, learners-focused teaching and learning bestows places more responsibility on the students themselves rather than the teacher. In this way, students not only develop writing skills based on reading but can also develop self-directed learning skills that can be used in the absence of a teacher.

Therefore, the relationship between reading and writing has become a k ey component of course design. However, the establishment of instructio nal strategies that best utilize the classroom environment to promote th e benefits of the reading-writing relationship is still in its early stages. A number of studies have investigated the selection of reading-writing t asks for classroom teaching; examples of these tasks include written sum maries, thematic analyses, oral retellings, and dramatizations, the latter of which involves working on a skit or drama, or rewriting a well-kno wn story from a different point of view (Lenski & Johns, 1997). Howev er, many of these activities are low in linguistic abilities since the provi ded texts come with vocabulary and sentence structure. Caudery (1998) also argued that students endeavor to understand the given text, make minor changes, and then see how the newly made text is different in meaning. Grabe (2004, p. 257) devised ten principles for activities that connected reading and writing in a language classroom. Five of these pr inciples are listed below.

1) Position matters: students and teachers work directly with tasks

2) Discussion: talk about texts and tasks based on personal anecdotes

3) Reading: interaction with texts

4) Nature of tasks: be realistic and not too difficult

5) Teacher support: assistance with tasks

According to McGinley (1992), reading-writing activities can be divided into the following four categories: (1) redesigning stories, (2) stylistic ref ormulation, (3)experimental syntax and reformulation, and (4) genre refo rmulation (pp. 231-233).Redesigning stories involves modifying the origi nal structure or background of a particular story. Stylistic reformulation incorporates teacher feedback as students go through the process of alte ring the linguistic features in their writing to make it sound more nati ve-like. Experimental syntax and reformulation is the practice of paraphr asing using different forms of grammar allowing students to be exposed to a diverse range of English sentences. Finally, in genre reformulation, students rewrite a given text for a different purpose and/or audiences.

According to recent reading-based writing research, how to read has a greater influence on how to write for second language learners. Due to of the structural and linguistic differences, students are not familiar with how or what to write (Tsang, 1996; Quinn, 2003). They are also not s ure about vocabulary, resource, metaphors, and connotations (Krashen, 1 993). Therefore, providing a certain topic and asking students to compo se their own writing is not always an effective strategy. In fact, student s taught in this way could develop undesirable writing habits that may be difficult to reverse at a later date (Cho & Krashen, 1994). Falk-R oss (@003) also argues that, if they do now keep studying, some stude nts forger what they learned in their English writing classes at time pa sses.

In response to the linguistic and structural limitations that EFL learners face when writing, many studies support reading-based writing instructio n in order to improve the acquisition of the target language in general and English writing skills in particular. For instance, Gao (2013) argues that they best way to teach EFL writing is to provide target writing sa mples with reading materials and have students practice based on these samples. As Quinn (2003) also suggested, in doing so students tend to mimic the linguistic pattern and structure of the provided reading in th eir writing, especially those students learning English as an L2. ue to t his, providing quality writing samples and illustrating how a native Eng lish speaker connects text to writing is crucial in EFL settings. Further more, Lin and Hui-Chuan (2001) argues that how students interpret an d internalize reading material is the key to successful writing. According to these authors, developing word identification skills through reading le ads to improve spelling and orthography in writing. They concluded tha t reading instruction is important in obtaining writing skills; that is to say, reading leads to better writing. Falk-Ross (2003) claimed that an i nstructional approach that uses the reading-writing connection in particu larly beneficial for the improvement of non-native students' English lang uage literacy. In the EFL environment, students first imitate and then l ater develop their own thoughts. While learning to write, students start to produce unique and meaningful content after a period of borrowing i deas and expressions from reading material.

Falk-Ross (2003) described specific improvement in students' writing as they progressed from writing a simple review and repeating certain phra ses to providing their own examples to support the main points of the text. Tsang (1996) also observed that "general knowledge [improvement through reading] had heped to develop content in writing" (p.228). Stu dents were exposed to proper models of "construction, agreement, tense, number, word order, and function" (p.228) that could strengthen and in fluence their use of language.

Other EFL reading-based writing studies have also established the benefi ts of the reading-based writing instruction. Cho and Krashen (1994) exa mined struggling students learning English as an L2 and found that th ey could make the transition to writing by reading light materials such as abridged and simplified versions of novels. Constantino, Lee, Cho, an d Krashen (1997) also showed that reading for pleasure increased the q uality of writing in a reading-based writing class at the college level. M anzo and Manzo's (2013) study of a reading-thinking inventory (a form of analytical reading that included reading the lines, reading between th e lines, and reading beyond the lines) found that the critical views stud ents expressed in writing on social issues developed over time, including improvements in personal and emotional responses, elaboration, cognitive thinking, and task engagement.

In the 1990s, based on the EFL reading-based writing instructional theo ry, colleges in Korea started to offer English for General Purposes (EG P) writing classes that focused on the improvement of communicative a bility. Mining as critical reading, rhetorical reading as analyzing, and th e modeling approach as close reading have been taught in English writi ng classes based on reading materials (Choi, 2000; Kim, 2004; Song & Park, 2004). However, as argued by Park (1997), writerly reading, whic h asks students to read as if they were the writer, and extensive and v oluntary reading have only recently gained attention English writing clas ses in Korea have shifted their focus away from the older way of writin g instruction (teaching writing divorced of reading) to the newly adopte d method, which encourages the learning writing knowledge naturally fr om reading content.

A number of studies have investigated writing classes in Korea that app ly reading-based writing instruction addressing the curricula teaching me thods, the unique nature of the Korean educational system. Park (1997) examined the attitudes of students and instructors towards writing classe s taught by native English speakers and found that students and instru ctors were mostly positive towards the program with a long-term progr am of at least three years preferable to a one year program. Furthermo re, third or fourth year students tended to be more motivated than tho se in their first or second years. In a similar vein, Kim (2004) investiga ted a cooperative English program whose instructors were a mix of nati ve and non-native speakers. In this program, the native instructors taug ht conversational courses while non-native instructors taught expression, vocabulary, reading, and writing. The results showed that the students' writing performance improved over the duration of the program.

Many colleges also offer intensive English writing programs during sum mer and winter holidays to substitute or complement regular semester writing programs. Given the number of major and elective courses stud ents are required to take during the regular semester, it is difficult for them to dedicate much time to the study of English writing (Cho, 200 2). If they do take an English writing course during the regular semest er, focused concentration on the subject is uncommon. Jung and Kim (2001) and Song and Park (2004) have thus claimed that short-term E nglish writing programs during semester breaks stimulate motivation. Fo r example, Cho (1998) reported the positive outcome of an intensive En glish writing program during the summer and winter breaks at a colleg e in Korea with students' confidence increasing alongside their writing p erformance.

In these regular and intensive English writing programs at Korean univ ersities, a number of instructional methods are used such as providing a range of reading material, using movies as audio-visual prompts, and pr omoting small group activities. Unlike English conversational courses, w hich are typically taught by native English speakers, English writing pro grams are often taught by Korean instructors in some colleges (Bang, 2 004; Kim, 2011; Lee, 1997; Park, 1993). In addition to the assigned t extbook, teachers tend to source external material suitable for their stud ents' level such as articles from reputed English magazines, the speeches of well-known public figures, and movie scripts. All of these are used i nside and outside the classroom as content for writing activities and assi gnments. For example, in the case of movies, students watch a movie s elected by the instructor and then write a story about it afterwards, oft en with a particular rhetorical focus. In their study of a college English program in Korea that used movies as input, Kim, Jung, Jang, and Eu m (1999) described the use of storyline summaries, ending rewrites, and characters modifications. Small group activities may also take many forms in the EFL writing classroom (Lim, 2006). For higher level students, stu dents may also peer-edit each other's writing in addition to receiving tea cher feedback. In other cases, students as a group will compose a writte n assignment together by assigning different sections to each member.

In addition to the curricula, administrative environment, and teaching m ethods, another important aspect to consider in English writing classes i n Korean colleges is the systematic situation. Many universities provide both a required EGP writing course for all students and elective writin g courses targeted for specific groups, such as engineering, business, and literature (Ahn, 2007; Lim, 2006; Sung, Pho, & Lee, 2004). Some colle ges employ an independent department to provide and oversee EGP an d elective writing classes; others have their English literature or English education departments take responsibility for these programs. Instructors fluent in both English and Korean are continuously required to staff th ese classes. Because of the learning styles and cultural factors unique to Korean students, exacerbated by the long-time practice of passive recepti on in English writing instruction in formal education, EGP writing instr uctors are expected to teach in English but at the same time provide u seful feedback and advice in Korean.

Textbooks designed specifically for Korean students learning English writ ing have been developed in some colleges. These textbooks are mostly r eading-based and try to connect the contents of the readings to writing activities (Jung & Kim, 2001). As such, teachers often need to create s eparate handouts for grammar points, vocabulary and idiomatic phrases, often assembled into a booklet of supplementary materials that is used by all teachers in the course (Choi, 2012). Booklets such as these usuall y cannot be used by other schools and are hard to generalize because t hey represent the specific characteristics and learning styles of the partic ular school from which they originate. However, this internal cooperatio n among instructors is a strategy that can improve students' writing pe rformance.

Furthermore, many colleges place their students in their EGP writing pr ogram according to proficiency level, though schools have different stand ards for this division (Jin, 2005; Kwon, 2002; Lee, 1998; Park, 1997; Park, 2003; Song & Park, 2004). Some consider TOEIC writing scores, some rely on writing scores from their own placement tests, and others even consider conversation ability or overall English scores not directly r elated to writing ability. Another trend in EGP at the university level i s to create a space in which English can be studied and practiced and the secretion of the student. Often going under a name like "English L ounge," these places tend to enforce a strict English only policy and pr ovide a wealth of English media to use as input, such as books, magazi nes and newspapers, with movies and TV programs (especially news pro grams like CNN TV) playing in the background. Computers are often made available to complete class homework. EGP instructors may be req uired to take turns overseeing the English lounge, where they have a ch ance to meet their students outside of the classroom. These types of lou nges have been mostly used for conversational purposes; however, guidan ce in and feedback on writing has also started to become a common fe ature. Students can bring their assignments in for written and oral feed back, and many writing-related books and helpful material are provided.

2.4 Intertextuality in Reading-Based Writing

2.4.1 Intertextuality

Intertextuality is defined the interrelationship of one text to other texts (Allen, 2011). When someone reads, they use their previous knowledge to help understand the content of the target text. This prior knowledge may include previous experiences reading similar content, regardless of whether the experience was positive or negative. Sterponi (2007) argued that a reader's imagination and expectations for the new content are also intertextual factors. The reading process reviews past information, receives present information, and mixes these to produce new information. Tomas(1999) added that reading texts in the context of intertextuality is a creative way to acquire knowledge by absorbing and transforming information. In other words, a particular text is not dependent but instead exists as part of an interactional relationship with all texts that have been read in the past. In this sense, readers are considered to be active meaning-makers (Worton, 1990). They are not looking for the main idea of one particular text, but establishing a variety of ideas sourced from numerous texts.

Intertextuality in an education context involves the relationships between reader and text, text and social-culture, and social-culture and reader (Shuart-Faris & Bloome, 2004). When a student reads a text, they consider its background such as the year the text was written, the traditions of the society the text originated from, and the culture the text seeks to portray. According to Green and Meyer (1991), by comprehending this background, a reader starts to understand the intention and purpose of the author, and what the text aims to say. In order to help such understanding, teachers usually provide background information before or after reading (Lewis, 2008). This approach is specially recommended in EFL as students are not exposed to the target culture in their daily lives. As an example, Lewis (2008) outlined a method to contextualize a text that focused on ordering a hamburger at McDonalds in the USA. Before the students start reading, the teacher could introduce the history of McDonalds, the menu, and how food is order. Since the students are not from the target country, the teacher could make additional comparisons between McDonalds and any famous fast food franchise in the students' native country. Providing additional information about the target culture enhances the students' understanding of the text, and they may compare the next text they read to their own social and cultural context without teacher guidance.

Another meaning of intertextuality is the relationship between texts in reading, in other words, the influence of the previous text on the next one, and on the others that follow (Egan-Robertson, 1998). If students are reading the chapters of a book in order, reading the first and second chapter separately is different from reading them in sequential order; the information students receive while reading the second text is different (Maloof, 2000). If they read and understand the first chapter, the knowledge they obtain can be applied to understanding the second chapter. However, if students read the second chapter without reading the first, the gaps in knowledge at the first chapter may have filled will remain. Qi (2005) also noted that if the first chapter is helpful for understanding the second, and the second is similarly helpful for the third, comprehension and internalization will improve as the students move through the chapters in sequential order. This is why arranging texts in the appropriate order is important for boosting reading competency.

2.4.2 The Effect of Intertextuality on EFL Reading

Considering intetextuality when teaching reading has been used an effec tive strategy in literature and language education for a number of reaso ns. First, it can increase student interest in the target language, leading them to become more active learners (Dinkelman, 2003; Liston & Zeich ner, 1990). Intertextual reading experiences improve learner confidence when a new text is introduced. The students will tend to consider previ ous related readings and eventually ascribe a new meaning to the prese nt one.Therefore, individual students may analyze the same text in diffe rent ways based on their reading and learning experiences. Second, inter textual reading helps students to provide a richer interpretation and exp lanation of a text (Holmes, 2004). The meaning of a target text is defi ned largely on knowledge gained from previously read texts written by the same author or based around similar topics. Third, intertextual readi ng expands students' cultural exposure and in doing so, leads to the m ore effective internalization of the target text because a stronger underst anding of the cultural background of the text naturally leads to a stron ger understanding of the content (Kuit, Reay, & Freeman, 2001). In su m, intertextual reading is not simply about receiving additional informat ion from other texts, but about creating new meaning.

In acknowledgment of the positive effects of using intertextuality in rea ding literary works, the educational field has also started to adopt this strategy to improve reading comprehension. In the EFL field in particul ar, where students face an initial language barrier, providing background schema (the primary meaning of intertextuality as used in this study) to reading material has been shown to stimulate the learning process (Chi, 1995). Although the provision of reference information for reading is fre quently used in EFL, the consideration of the order of individual texts i n relation to their themes (the second meaning of intertextuality used i n this study) has not been as readily adopted (Lemke, 1992). Some rea ding comprehension research has considered intertextual order, but most reading-based writing studies have not provided much input, and they have not clearly defined what order the input should follow.

Reading materials in EFL writing generally consists of authentic sample s, so the first aim is to offer students various genres of text with a ran ge of content.Mungthaisong (2003) recommended that students be expos ed to the target culture in a variety of situations. Morgan (2008) provi ded an example of teaching reading in relation to intertextual order. Th e author says that if students read about an accident that happened at a grocery store the previous week, and another at an airport that week, each reading is not closely related to nor displaces the similar situation. After students read about grocery shopping, they have to refresh and pr epare to read a text about an airport scene. If the activity was truly in tertextual, a reading about cooking in the kitchen would come after the grocery shopping rather than the one set at the airport. Grocery shoppi ng and cooking at home are more directly related to each other than g rocery shopping and the airport. In this way, the knowledge and infor mation learned from the previous chapter could be used and connected to understand the next chapter.

Based on these advantages, the two meanings of intertextuality in EFL reading will now be described further. According to Chi (1998), intertex tuality as background schema provides students with objective informatio n in order to allow for a better understanding of the target text. Mean while, the intertextual order of each text lets students actively create m eaning as they read (Myers, 1993). Nielsen (1998) added that a student who better understands and internalizes the first chapter of a set of tex ts will better comprehend the second chapter. In summary, the first me aning of intertextuality involves objective explanation, while the second i s based on a subjective learning experience.

Background schema for EFL reading allows the content of the target te xt to be recognized and analyzed from different perspectives. Abasi and Akbari (2008) explained that readers can identify sections that they do not understand and locate missing information that will aid in understa nding themselves during this process. In addition, Wang and Wang (20 06) argued that background schema includes linguistic information such as new vocabulary and content concerns such as action or behavior that may be considered unusual in the students' native culture. The authors suggested that not knowing the meaning of certain words or phrases ca n sometimes prevent students from ever fully comprehending the underl ying intention of some texts.

The benefits of reading in intertextual order are the repetition of learni ng and the opportunity to apply the content to the context to a learne r's life. According to Atkinson (2008), when reading a new chapter, the learning from the previous chapters is repeated so that this cumulative knowledge is re-invoked. Improving writing performance means developi ng an understanding of the function and use of the written word (Gui- ying, 2006). This understanding is enabled by repeated practice; in fact, constant exposure to a narrow range of material is more effective than exposure to many different texts. In addition, as suggested by Lingling and Jingjin (2009), the true meaning of learning is not limited to unde rstanding texts, it is also includes the application of this understanding to daily life. When the knowledge derived from prior chapter is applied to subsequent chapter by a reader, who then notes any similarities betw een this new knowledge and their real life, the learning process become s valuable.

In Korea, intertextual reading education should consider cultural influenc es. Choi (2007) claimed that, due to the nature of the school system a nd the prevailing teaching style, Korean students are adept at receiving information but weak at creating new ideas in an educational context. The concept of intertextuality in Korea includes neither the criticism of texts, nor the constructions of a new understanding; instead, it is the o ne-way reception of texts by students with the teacher often explaining the content directly (Yoo, 2008). If the background schema provides stu dents with additional information, reviewing the knowledge from a prior chapter and applying it to a subsequent chapter can help prompt self-in terpretation and the creation of new concepts (Allen, 2011; Tomas, 199 9). Thus, while the primary meaning of intertextual reading might be e asier for Korean students to understand than its secondary meaning, bot h meanings of intertextuality are encouraged for improved reading comp rehension.

2.4.3 Intertextuality and Cognitive Processes in Reading and Writing

The cognitive process involves critical thinking skills (Eckoff, 1993; Tier ney & Shanahan, 1996). Grabe (2003) explained that both reading and writing require meaning to be negotiated, reading with the author, and writing with the readers. For authors, the cognitive processes used in re ading turn out to similar to those used in writing including the gatheri ng of ideas, questioning, hypothesizing, planning, drafting, aligning, revi sing, monitoring meaning, assuming, using schemata, making meta-com ments citing evidence, validating, generating ideas, formulating meaning, and evaluating. From a linguistic perspective, as proposed by Olson an d Lang (2008), both reading and writing are based on perspective, pho nemes, the semantic system, and long-term and short-term memory. In other words, the two skills are considered to share similar cognitive cha racteristics (Chi, 1999).

Ferris and Roberts (2001, p.170) identified three dimensions of cognitive processing in reading-writing: (1) cognitive, (2) textual, and (3) personal. In the cognitive dimension, both readers and writers use prior knowledg e in achieving their task. They set a purpose before they start and they seek help if something is not clear during the reading or writing, inclu ding asking questions or searching for answers online. In the textual di mension, both readers and writers communicate with the text. Readers t ry to understand the main idea while writers try to convey the theme as clearly as possible. For the personal dimension, the individual motiati on for reading and/or writing, the level of engagement, learners' identiti es as readers and/or writers, and the goals of the learning are importan t considerations.

2.5 Reflective Reading

2.5.1 Advantages of Reflective Strategies in EFL Learning

Reflective methods are frequently used in teacher training and language education across different fields (Akinbode, 2013). According to Alger (2 006), reflective reading helps self-regulation, allows individual performa nce to be monitored, and modifies behavior, weaknesses, and motivation. Furthermore, reflection involves understanding, oneself, reviewing the con text, and the communication process with oneself. Hagevik, Aydeniz, an d Rowell (2012) also argues that reflective learning helps to develope a critical view of the material being learnt. In doing so, language compet ency increase. Their study demonstrated that students who practice readi ng in a reflective manner with teacher guidance are able to do the sam e on their own at a later point in time. Go (2012) also claimed that t eaching students reflective reading is a way of developing language lear ning skills as well as helping them to engage in self-directed learning b y promoting learner autonomy. Therefore, these studies contend that refl ection involved the transfer from teacher-regulated learning to a self-reg ulated process.

In addition to conscious reflective learning and associated strategies, read ing tself is a genuinely self-reflective process. Levin and Camp (2005) e xplained that readers develop self-awareness, perspective, and an underst anding of their values while reading; thus, reading can foster the proces s of self-definition. Tok and Dolapcioglu (2013) also stated that reading is a method to realize oneself within the text and what students read a nd contemplate in class contributes to their growth in language ability. In their study, students made connections between the content in a giv en text and their personal experiences while reading; i.e., they reflect u pon their lives through text. It can then be said that reading is a trans actional process between the text and its readers'own lives. Lambe, Mc Nair, and Smith (2013) intrpduced reflective journaling as another way of reflective reading. It is known to increase self-perception in reading a nd writing. As a method of self-directed study, it suits students who ne ed to continue their English education once their academic courses have finished. A reflective journal can improve writing skills by reflecting th e contexts and lookng back on their learning experience.

As mentioned above teaching EFL reading in a reflective manner is an attempt to move the control of literacy from the teacher to students. I n a study by Gibson (2010) on reflective-reading in teacher training, st udents were able to use the learnt strategy on their own after training. After an explanation and the modeling of reflective skills by the teache r, students started to independently question and apply these skills on t

heir own. According to the reader response theory of Ryder (2013), hel
ping readers to engage their own experiences when interacting with rea
ding materials is crucial. Guiding readers to respond and react to a tex
t on their own is a method of self-reflection. When students make con
nections between the text and their lives, they tend to understand the
text on a deeper level. Besides, Beach (1990) has also argued that in t
he process of writing about their experiences based on reading, students
can define each moment of a particular experience as well as acknowled
ge the meaning of each experience in the long-term. Chamblee (2003,
p. 372) showed that this process of reflection in reading and writing is
connected to an individual's personal life (Figure 2).

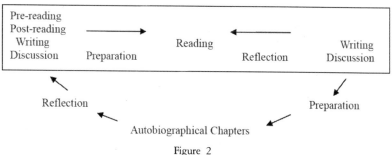

Figure 2
Reflection in Reading-Writing (Chamblee, 2003, p.372)

2.5.2 Reflective-Reading Instruction in EFL

In order to achieve success in reading-based writing, students are encour
aged to study the relationship between reading and writing. One of the
most effective ways of doing this is through reflective-reading strategies
(Casazza, 2003). According to Pedro, Abodeeb-Gentile, and Courtney (2
012), writing a summary of reading is a good reflective-reading strategy
and a crucial skill in critical thinking as it involves selecting important

information from the text and omitting unnecessary details. Summary w riting facilitated the recall of information from a text in order to raise questions and provoke discussion (Kitchakarn, 2012). Since writing a su mmary review enables what has just been learned to be reviewed and r eflected on its frequent use in the language classroom as a reflective m ethod is to be expected.

A reflective journal is another effective activity based on reflective-readin g instruction in EFL (Warin et al, 2006). Kelly and Farnan(1991) prop osed that this strategy connects a text to a student's own thinking. By reading journals, students develop an awareness of the reading process a nd reflect on what they have found interesting in the text. Reflective jo urnals also provide students with critical engagement, encourage reflectio n on past experiences, and all the recall of prior knowledge in the read ing process (El-Hindi, 2003). The transactional view argues that reflectiv e reading and reacting to what is read help students create transactions between the text and themselves, eventually enabling them to achieve a higher order of thinking (Washbourne, 2012).

Another frequently used method in reflective reading strategy is group activities (King & Kitchener, 1994). After reviewing the content throug h summarization and a reading journal entry, students can apply the co ntent to their personal lives. In this process, a learner may find it diffic ult to access related past experiences. Therefore, Collins (1998) used gro up activities and discussion in order to facilitate brainstorming for writin g. In doing so, students can come up with their own writing topics rat her than use the ones provided by the teacher. In most cases, teachers tend to propose a selection of writing topics related to the reading in t he first half of the semester, while in the second half, students are enc ouraged to choose their own, either as a group or individually (Kuo, 20 12). Discussion with classmates benefits learning by encouraging behavio

r such as listening to others' perspectives, rethinking one's own viewpoi
nt, and creating new ways of thinking, as a result, students are encour
aged to discuss writing assignments with each other (Tomcho 2012). In
this way, reflective language teaching acknowledges the positive effect of
group discussion.

2.6 Teacher Feedback

2.6.1 Advantages of Teacher Feedback

The social perspective of reading focuses on the intentions of the teache
r and students as they jointly produce meaning (Abrams & Gerber, 201
3; Shintani & Ellis, 2013). Teachers are facilitators and guides leading s
tudents to improve their literacy level providing examples of the target
learning style and construction of meaning before and after the student
s' engage in training and practice (Kucan & Beck, 1997). In the develo
pment of learning proficiency, Casazza (2003) claimed that the reaction
of and feedback from an expert is crucial; in particular, regular, repeate
d, and guided conversational interaction between teacher and student is
an effective means of improving writing. Kim (2012) stated that it ther
e was no direct feedback from the teacher, students would not know w
hether their content and structure was appropriate.For the target form o
f writing. Motivating and improving student reflection on the reading-w
riting connection involves more than merely having them write reading
journals in and after class; rather, the process requires teacher feedback
at the appropriate time and in the appropriate manner. Reflective readin
g and writing activities that are characterized by abundant feedback fro
m teachers and their subsequent writing performance is likely to improv
e more quickly.

Two types of teacher feedback have proved useful for students with low language proficiency: written feedback and oral feedback (Berg, 1999; B itchener, Young, & Cameron, 2005; Carson & Nelson, 1994; Ferris, 20 03; Ferris & Hedgcock, 2005). Written feedback is the more traditional way of providing professional advice helping students reflect on their mi stakes and the second round of the learning process. Ferris and Hedgco ck (2005, pp. 262-263) introduced the following principles of written fe edback.

1. Teachers need to respond to every single problem on every single dr aft.

2. Teachers should take care to avoid taking over a student's text. Fina l decisions about content and revision should be left

in control of the writer.

3. Feedback should focus on the issue presented by each individual stud ent and their paper, not on rigid presciptions.

4. Teachers should treat their students as individuals, considering writte n feedback as part of an ongoing conversation between themselves and each individual students writer.

5. Teachers should provide both encouragement and constructive criticis m in their feedback.

The first two principles explain the teacher's role in providing feedback. The first indicates that any mistakes left uncommented on in a draft w ill be assumed by the writer to be correct, and thus they are likely to repeat the mistake next time. The second principle is based on the idea that the teacher can provide feedback but the choice to accept it should be left to be students, a method of guidance that bestows more responsibilities on the student regarding their learning. The third and fourth principles highlight the importance of acknowledging the individual characteristics and personality of each student. Although the English language and individual classroom curriculum have rules that every student has to follow, the teacher should also consider differences between students in their learning and the way they express themselves. If students recognize that the teacher is attempting to address their different needs, the feedback will be likely to be more effective. The fifth and last principle is crucial, especially for students' at a low-proficiency level. They tend to be apprehensive about handing in their work to the teacher and receiving feedback. If the teacher gently points out their mistakes by advising directions for revisions, they are more likely to understand the true propose of teacher feedback and follow the advice.

Hyland (2003) also pointed out that too much teacher feedback can overwhelm students and decrease their motivation. He advised teachers to provide opinions about overall organization and content in the first draft. Grammar mistakes and other small errors can be pointed out in the final draft, which will not influence the content. Feedback for the final draft shuold be based on the feedback for earlier drafts. In addition, teacher feedback should be individualized for each student because they have different learning styles and characteristics (Ferris, 2003).

Written feedback can be provided through commentary, rubrics, and correction codes. Commentary can be either written in the margin or given at the end of the submission (Ferris, 2003; Hyland & Hyland, 2001; Nation, 2009). As summarized by Hyland (1998), comments in the mar gin can be more conversational and point out target problem areas, wh ereas end comments can be longer and provide an overall reaction. A r ubric, which is more often used for the final draft rather than earlier d rafts, provides a more objective guideline, with scores given for the diffe rent components of writing; students can therefore easily see the areas where improvement is needed (Grabe & Kaplan, 1998). The third feedb ack strategy, error correction codes, helps to improve self-correction skill s. These codes, which should be discussed with the students before feed back occurs, specify the location and type of error but do not provide t he correction itself, thus promoting students' self-editing and self-revision skills (Ferris, 2003). In using any of these methods, the feedback should be detailed and clear to ensure student understanding, especially in the EFL environment.

Oral feedback from the teacher and to individual students is often provi ded during what is called a learning conference (Williams, 2005). The most significant advantages of this conference is the opportunity to exch ange opinions, negotiate meaning, and discuss the student's learning pro cess. Patthey-Chavez and Ferris (1997,pp. 82-83) listed the following ad vantages of oral conferences:

1. Potential for interaction and negotiation

2. Clear up misunderstandings for the teacher regarding the student's in tended meaning and for the students regarding teacher feedback

3. Provide more focused and usable comments than does written feedba ck

4. Offer a more effective means of communication for auditory learners

5. Allow students a chance to raise questions on written feedback

6. Develop learner autonomy

7. Help students construct a revision plan

8. Save the teacher's time spent on the marking of papers

An oral conference can offer a chance for a student to explain the purpose and meaning of their writing. The teacher is therefore not forced to guess and provide feedback that may be at odds with what the writer intended, but can instead discuss it with the student. In addition, unlike written feedback, oral conferences provide a student with the chance to explain themselves, which will naturally improve their ability to develop rewriting plans. This is because students feel more responsible for their revision work than when they are simply assigned to do it by the teacher.

Oral feedback can therefore provide suitable guidelines for each student whatever their cultural, educational, and linguistic background (Mendonca & Johnson, 1994; Truscott, 1996). According to Nelson and Carson (1998), students can record or write down what has been discussed in the conference for a later use and review. For students who are nervous or uncomfortable talking to the teacher one-on-one, two or more students can come in a group. Students should also be allowed to skip the conference, should they so wish; the learning is in the hands of the students themselves, not the teacher. Students may not be aware of the ora l conference and the associated expectations should be communicated bef ore conferences are scheduled. Students should be encouraged to be acti ve and teachers should start the conference by asking questions about a ny written feedback that was unclear. Teachers are advised to avoid dir ect advice and comment; rather, it is better to ask about the student's intentions and opinions about the learning content. The discussion could also begin with complements to lower tension, move on to how learnin g could be improved, and then end with praise.The final decisions abou t revisions and whether to follow the teacher feedback should be the st udents' own (Min, 2006).

2.6.2 Need for Teacher Feedback in EFL

The effect of feedback is even greater in an EFL setting (Caruso, 2011; Lam, 2013; Miao, 2006). According to Enginarlar (1993), teacher feedb ack is crucial in language learning especially in EFL. For upper-level EF L students, feedback from classmates and from themselves (i.e., revising their own work) is also valuable, but for lower-level EFL students, until they obtain a certain level of language competence, only teacher feedbac k is recommended. This is because low-level EFL students are often not able to find their own mistakes, and may give incorrect advice to other students.

Above all, EFL students are not confident in dealing with the target la nguage; their confidence comes from the teacher's praise and encourage ment (Matsumura & Hann, 2004). Cohen and Cavalcanti (1990) also ar gued that positive reaction from the teacher would also produce better results. One reason to provide feedback is to enhance students' motivati on for learning. If teachers take the time to respond to each student's reflective journal, this regular communication with an expert would pro mote more effective reflective thinking. Cross (1999) also mentioned tha t the teacher's reaction plays a central role in classroom assessment, esp ecially with regard to students''reflective abilities. Sadler (1998) added th at students'' reflective abilities can be improved through judicious teache r input.

In EFL, both written and oral feedback is recommended. Ferris (1999) contended that if the teacher uses written comments, they should be wr itten clearly. Some students with a low level of language competence h ave a hard time reading criticisms in English. Hirvela and Du (2013) a rgued that an oral conference might be a burden for those whose speak ing proficiency is insufficient. In this case, an interpreter can be of hel p. In addition to these issues, many EFL students tend to assume that all teacher comments are correct so they should endeavor to address all of them (Leki, 1991). Therefore, the teacher should guide students to ta ke responsibility for their learning and let them know that teacher feed back is only one opinion; students should instead makeindependent decisi ons on whether or not to follow the teacher's advice (Chandler, 2003).

Another aspect to consider about teacher feedback in EFL writing classe s is whether to provide feedback on students' linguistic problems, and if so, how much of this type of feedback is appropriate. Many scholars po int out that direct error correctiois not effective (Fathman & Whalley, 1 990; Ferris & Roberts, 2001; Franzen, 1995). Fathman and Whalley (1 990) claimed that students usually follow the teacher's comments, and c hange their way of learning accordingly. For this reason, teachers should understand the current level of each student's linguistic ability and prov ide guidelines that address the target picture. For example, as Truscott's study (1996) on error correction established, teachers can write phrases s uch as, "Please look for subject-verb disagreement, and watch out for c apitalization" at the end of reading reflections rather than pointing out every grammatical mistake and making corrections with a differently col ored pen. Indirect feedback such as this can provide students with time to think about their own errors and help them develop self-correction s kills.

2.7. Type of Writing Education in EFL

In EFL writing classrooms, three types of composition are commonly emp loyed: a) controlled writing, b) guided writing, and c) free writing (Silva, 1990). The first type is usually used in junior and high schools, focusing on the correctness of individual sentences and repeated practice, and leadi ng to the one particular answer expected by the teacher (Zemach, 2009). Activities commonly associated with this instructional method include cop ying, reproduction, recombination, matching, and filling in the blanks.

The two other types are more common at the college level. Guided wri ting refers to composition in which students model a given format prov ided by a teacher with their own choices of vocabulary and phrases (Re nshaw, 2007). The content is restricted while the linguistic features are left open to the students. Guided writing provides evidence of the lingu istic ability of the students; therefore, it is also called semi-communicati on (Williams, 2005). This type of writing includes descriptive, informati onal, and explanative compositions, all of which have the writer present an objective perspective. Well-known examples of this type of writing i nclude describing a picture or photo, informing someone about a matter for which the writer has specific information, and explaining a situation. Free writing where students write on a given topic using their own tho ughts and logic (Zemach & Rumisek, 2003). Students are able to use a ny vocabulary and phrases they choose as in guided writing, but they must also express their own ideas. Free writing includes opinionated, ar gumentative, and assertive compositions that highlight the subjective per spective of the writer (Lambert, 2008). Well-known examples of this ty pe of writing include arguing for or against one side of a controversial issue, insisting upon a change in public policy, and persuading someone to change their opinion on a topic.

2.8 Self-Awareness in EFL Learning

According to Ellis (1994), success in the acquisition of a foreign langua ge and the speed at which it can be done depends on learner self-awar eness. In other words, a learner who recognizes the importance of learni ng the target language is motivated more in their studies and learns fa ster than one who does not. Other scholars, such as Elbro and Petersen (2004) and Saito (2007), also discussed the impact of self-awareness on learning in EFL. In the study, the researchers concluded that self-aware ness helps learners to acquire a variety of complementary learning skills. The latter study suggested that students have a definite reason to learn a foreign language and a precise understanding of what to study impro ved further and more quickly than other studies did.

Past research has investigated the effect of student's self-awareness on E FL listening, reading, and writing learning. Cross (2012) examined the e ffect of awareness on improving listening skills, while Zhang (2001) ana lyzed its effect on EFL students' reading comprehension. Ruan (2013), who examined the same effect in writing development, showed that Chi nese EFL students' self-awareness in relation to writing type, genre, and different areas helped them to perform better in composition after the e xperiment. By considering the nature of the writing, the writing strateg ies available, and themselves as writers, learners were able to think mor e deeply and broadly during the study. Negretti (2012) also found that self-awareness in academic writing positively influences task-perception a nd self-regulation in EFL students. A similar study by Hidi and Boscolo (2006) concluded that the development of self-awareness in EFL writing leads to evaluated self-efficacy and writing motivation.

2.9 Self-Confidence in EFL Learning

As with self-awareness, self-confidence in EFL learning is also crucial du e to the language barrier. Dornyei (2001) described self-confidence as th e belief that one has the ability to produce results accomplish goals or perform tasks completely. Norman and Hyland (2003) identified three e lements of confidence in language learning: 1)cognitive confidence, whic h refers to a learner's knowledge of their ability 2)performative confiden ce, which is the learner's ability to act 3) emotional confidence, which r efers to the learner's comfort regarding the first two elements. Therefor e, confidence in learning means that a learner should be able to recogni ze their ability, apply learned knowledge, and feel emotionally secure in these aspects. It has been found, however, that EFL students' learning c onfidence is generally lower than that of L1 students' due to linguistic difficulties, and their level of self-confidence strongly influences their suc cess or failure in language learning (Harmer, 2001). Additionally, a stud y by Eldred (2002) on EFL students' self-confidence argued that those who have higher confidence levels gain more opportunities. They also st ated that these students believed in their ability, and awareness of this needed to be incorporated into a teacher's classroom instruction.

CHAPTER III

METHODOLOGY

This study explores how reading-based writing instruction using intertext ual and reflective-reading strategies with teacher feedback (IRRF) influen ces the writing development of students. It was carried out in the requi red EGP writing courses taught by the researcher at a college in Kore a. The students in the EGP writing classes were divided into two exper imental groups and one control group. This chapter summarizes the foll owing assessments: a) the impact of IRRF reading-based writing instruct ion on test of writing performance, b) the strategies used in ten exposit ory texts, and c) a retrospective composing-process survey in addition to the measurement of self-confidence in writing. The experiment was cond ucted over a 16-week period in the fall semester of the 2013 academic year.

3.1 Research Design

The purpose of the present study was to examine the relationship betw een choice of writing instruction and Korean EFL students' writing deve lopment. The experiment took three forms as shown in Table 1: a) tra ditional comprehension questions consisting of short, multiple choice, an

d true or false answers, b) reading-base dreflective-reading strategies wit
h teacher feedback (RRF), and c) reading-based intertextual and reflectiv
e-reading strategies with teacher feedback (IRRF).

Group	Writing Instruction		Intervention
	Intertextual	RRF reading-based	
control	not used	not used	traditional instruction
RRF	not used	used	RRF reading-based
IRRF	used	used	IRRF reading-based

Table 1
Research Design

3.2 Subjects

The participants of this study were second-year college students from thre
e different English composition classes taught by the researcher at a univ
ersity in Korea. The general required English program for undergraduate
at the university included an English conversation course in the first year
and the writing course in the second year. The writing classes were 3 cr
edit courses, each consisting of two 75-minute classes per week. The stud
ents were placed in the writing program based on their final scores in th
e conversation course the previous year, which was not considered sufficie
nt to accurately measure the students' writing ability prior to the experi
ment. Therefore, a pre-test of students' writing level was conducted for t
he current study. A questionnaire answered on the first day of class reve
aled that the participants' TOEIC score averaged as the followings: a) co
ntrol group was around 482, b) RRF group was around 398, andc) IRRF

group was around 471. The three groups were all together averaged arou
nd 450 at the time of the experiment.

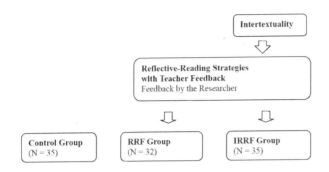

Figure 3
Characteristics of the Three Experimental Groups

A total of 102 students were divided into three groups: a control grou
p (N=35), a RRF group (N=32), and IRRF group (N=35). The stude
nts were aged between 20 and 24 and represented a range of majors i
ncluding social sciences, Korean literature, engineering, business, math, a
nd biology. In the control group 82.9% (N=29) were male and 17.1%
(N=6) were female. In the RRF group 75% (N=24) were male and 2
5% (N=8) were female. In the IRRF Group 60% (N=21) were male
and 40% (N=14) were female.

3.2.1 Control Group

The control group did not receive IRRF reading-based writing instruction;
however, they read and answered comprehension questions, consisting of sho
rt answers, multiple choice, and true-or-false statements, related to the text
book content. These questions have been used as a part of EGP course inst
ruction since 2007, and so were selected for use with the control group to
compare with the instructional strategies of the two experimental groups.

The students were first to asked to pre-read the text on their own befo re each chapter was covered in class. Then, on the first day of the lect ure for each chapter, the instructor played an audio DC of the main co ntent. While listening to the CD, the students who ha dread the mater ials at least once before the lecture were asked to close their books and concentrate on listening to remind themselves of the main ideas in the reading. The students who had not had the chance to read beforehand were asked to open the textbook and follow along with the CD. The i nstructor then explained the main theme of each chapter with a Power Point presentation (see Appendix A for a sample PPT lecture.)

The differences between the control and the two experimental groups oc curred after the PowerPoint explanation. The students in the control gr oup were asked to answer the comprehension question. There were six s hort answer questions for each chapter related to the content of the rea ding (see Appendix B for example short answer questions). After the st udents completed these, they volunteered to come to the board and wri te their answers. After an answer for each question had been written o n the board, the instructor went over them with the whole class. The s tudent who answered the first one read the question first and his or he r answer. The instructor then let the students know whether the answe r was correct.

For the multiple choice questions, the students read each sentence accor ding to their setting position and filled in the blank space with the cor rect multiple choice answer (see Appendix C for a sample of multiple c hoices questions and true-false statements). After reading the sentences t hey repeated the letter that represented the correct answer once more f or clarification. For the true/false statements, the students continued to read the given sentences for each questions and selected either "true" or "false" at the end. Because the teacher selected students when they wer e no volunteers for the short answers, and went around the class to ch eck the answers for the multiple choice and true/false questions, teacher -centered reading-based writing instruction was applied to the control gr oup.

3.2.2 Experimental Group

The procedure for the reflective-reading strategy training used in the cu rrent study was modified from the teaching instruction reported in Mac aro's (2006) study on language learning. Before the students practiced t he reflective-reading strategies, an explanation of its nature, importance, and purpose were provided to the students by the teacher. The three re flective-strategies used in the study were (1) summarizing the reading c ontent, (2) writing a reading journal, and (3) group discussion. Accordin g to Rudman (2013), (2013), one of the most valuable effects of reflect ive learning is promoting self-directed learning and self-motivation. As s uch, the teaching method used for the two experimental groups stood i n contrast to that used for the control group in that the reflective-readi ng strategies represented a student centered approach. Both experimental groups (the RRF and IRRF groups) used the three reflective-reading stra tegies accompanied by teacher feedback, but intertextuality in the readin g texts was only applied to the second experimental group (the IRRF g roup).

3.3 Instruments

To examine the impact of IRRF reading-based writing instruction on wr iting development, this study used the following instruments. Students t ook both objective and subjective pre- and post-writing tests. After bot h tests, the students participated in a retrospective composing-process su rvey and also reported their confidence in English writing.

3.3.1 Writing Proficiency Test

The participants of the current study strived to improve their English w riting skills in order to be able to fulfill work tasks following college g raduation. Therefore, a combination of modified TOEIC and TOEFL wri ting tests were used to assess student writing performance in this study because these tests are considered to be standard measures of English ability in relation to its used in work environment (see Appendices D a nd E for the pre- and post- writing tests). Both the TOEIC and TOEF L writing tests indicate objective and subjective writing sections (Lichten stein & Kimel, 2013; Min, 2006). The objective writing section requires that the students read or listen to certain facts and organize them into writing without providing an opinion. THe subjective wiritng section re quires that the students state an opinion on a controversial issue with s upporting evidence.

TOEIC"s objective writing task ⁻ a picture description for which only o ne sentence is evaluated ⁻ and the TOEFL"s objective task ⁻ reading an d listening to a lecture an producing five paragraphs ⁻ were combined and modified in this study to create the objective writing task. The stu dents were given a picture that presented a certain situation and were asked to describe it. The second writing task, the subjective type, was t o state and opinion with supporting evidence on a controversial issue. T he questions in the pre- and post-writing tests were different but were in the same forma and aimed at the same proficiency level. This study limited the students' pre- and post-writing tests to one paragraph (abou t 100-120 words), as the subjects did not have enough ability to comp ose more than one coherent paragraph of writing at the time of the ex periment. However, a single paragraph is still substantial enough to be evaluated as a composition (Reppen, 2002; Yoon & Lee, 2014).

3.3.2 Survey on Self-Awareness and Self-Confidence in Englis h Writing

A retrospective composing-process survey was used to examine the stude nts' self-awareness in writing and whether it had increased after the exp eriment. A high rating in self-awareness means that the students pay at tention to what they are writing. According to Kutney (2007), if learne rs care more and think deeply while writing, their finished product ten ds to be better in quality. The survey questions in the present study w ere adapted from the ones used in Cui's (2010) study. The retrospective composing-process involves looking back at one's writing process. It com plements the reflective-reading strategy instruction due to the similar ch aracteristics the two share with regard to reviewing. The retrospect com posing-process method was used to establish whether the students were th inking about the following fie components while writing: content, organiza tion, grammar, vocabulary, and punctuation. The rating was made one a 4-point Likert scale with 0 representing strongly disagree, and 4 strongly agree. The students also rated their self-confidence on the same scale with 0 meaning very confident, and 4 meaning not confident at all. Many pr evious studies have argued that a high-level of self-confidence is especially helpful for EFL learners studying composition (Pajares & Johnson, 1993; P ajares, 1994; Sasaki, 2000; Sasaki & Hirose, 1996). The students participa ted in the retrospective composing-process survey and the self-measureme nt of confidence after both the pre-a and post-tests (see Appendix F).

3.3.3 Texts

Ten expository texts were chosen for this study from an EFL reading-ba sed writing textbook by Broukal (2010). According to Montelongo and Hermandez (2007), reading an expository text heps the reader to organi ze their ideas so that they can be put into writing. Readability tests w ere performed on the texts in order to make sure that they were suitab le for students (Table 2).

Text	Level	Flesch	Gunning Fog	Flesch-Kindcaid	Coleman-Liau	SMOG	Auto	Linsear Write
1	Easy	75.6	9.4	6.8	8	6.4	7.8	8.4
2	Fairly Easy	75.0	6.7	4.5	7	5.2	4.5	5.9
3	Fairly Easy	68.3	8.6	6.7	11	6.6	7.4	6.2
4	Fairly Easy	67.0	7.5	6.3	9	6.4	5.2	5.0
5	Easy	79.5	6.1	4.9	8	5.0	4.8	5.1
6	Easy	77.6	7.8	5.6	8	5.8	5.3	6.2
7	Fairly Easy	74.7	8.3	5.7	8	6.6	5.0	6.0
8	Standard	78.0	5.9	5.1	7	5.6	3.9	5.4
9	Standard	74.5	7.4	6.2	8	5.8	5.8	6.6
10	Standard	79.5	6.1	5.4	6	4.3	4.3	6.0

Table 2

Readability of the Texts Used in the Study

The ten texts had an average readability rating of 74,.97 on the Flesch Reading Ease test, 7.38 on the Gunning Fog, 6.23 on the Flesch-Kinca id grade level, 8 on the Coleman-Liau Index, 5.77 on the SMOG Inde x, 5.4 on the Automated Readability Index, and 6.08 on the Linsear Write Formula, of the ten texts selected, three were easy to read, five were fairly easy, and two were standardly easy. These ratings meant the texts were appropriate for students of low-intermediate proficiency as we re the subjects of this study (see Appendix G for a sample of the textb ook). The school at which the study was conducted decided in a teache rs' meeting that the textbook would be appropriate for teaching EFL re ading-based writing for the following three reasons: (1) combined readin g and writing activities well, (2) the content was interesting for the stu dent, and (3) it provided systematic steps for the learning of writing.

3.4 Administrative Procedures for the Experiment

3.4.1 Instructional Procedure for the First Week

At the beginning of the semester, four procedures were carried out. Firs t, in order to determine the students' writing proficiency level before the experiment, a pre-writing test was administrated to the three groups. Sec ondly, a retrospective composing-process survey assessing the writing awa reness of the students was conducted. Students were also asked to self-re port their confidence in English writing. Finally, the students wrote their TOEIC scores on the survey if they had one (Table 3). Students did not have a TOEIC score were not included in the study.

Stage	Description	Purpose
1	pre-writing test	to examine the students' writing proficiency
2	retrospective composing-process survey	to assess the students' English composition awareness
3	self-measurement of confidence in English writing	to assess the students' confidence in English writing
4	survey of TOEIC score	to collect a standardized English test score before the experiment

Table 3
Procedures at the Beginning of the Semester

3.4.2 Instructional Procedure from the Second to the Fifteenth Weeks

Intertextuality in reading, implemented only in the IRRF Group, was pr ovided by the designed order of the textbook. Therefore, the control an d the RRF groups were assigned individual readings in a different order than how they were presented in the textbook, which meant they were not intertextuality related. Thus, while the three groups used the same textbook, the order of learning was different (Table 4).

IRRF Group	Control&RRF Groups
Chapter 1	Chapter 2
Chapter 2	Chapter 1
Chapter 3	Chapter 6
Chapter 4	Chapter 5
Chapter 5	Chapter 7
Chapter 6	Chapter 4
Chapter 7	Chapter 3
Chapter 8	Chapter 10
Chapter 9	Chapter 9
Chapter 10	Chapter 8

Table 4

Intertextuality: Order of the Textbook Chapters in the Three Groups

In addition to intertextual order, the IRRF group also received extra inf ormation as per the background schema component of intertextuality instruction which was discussed in the literature review (Chapter 2). The group was explained of the background schema for each chapter as part of the instructor's PowerPoint presentation for the reading contents.

The students in the two experimental groups utilized three reflective tas ks during the course: summarization, writing a reading journal, and gro up discussion. Students were provided with two handouts, one for sum marization and other for writing a reflection in their reading journal, aft er studying each chapter (see Appendices H and I for examples). After c ompleting these, the students were placed in small groups for discussion. The summarization and reading journal questions from the handouts for the first chapter were completed in class with the instructor providing model examples. The students were first taught summarization skills bef ore starting the summarization handout, such as deleting unnecessary se ntences, phrases, leaving only the essential information that best represe nts the main idea. After studying each chapter, students were given a handout of summarization as homework. In the next class, the students came to the whiteboard and wrote their answers on it followed by the whole class going through these answers together. If any student had a summary that differed from the ones written on the board, they could inquire about their sentences after class .

Upon completing the handouts, the students handed them in for teache r comments. The teacher looked through each of them and wrote feedb ack accordingly. Rather than directly correcting incorrect answers, the te acher underlined them and let the students think about modifying their re sponses themselves. For the remaining summary handouts for the other cha pters, the students completed them during the class period or finished the m as homework, depending on how much time each student required.

Following the teacher's PowerPoint explanation and the summary activit y, the students were then given the second handout about the reading journal. The handout contained reflective questions related to the studen t's experience reading the chapter in question. The questions invluded, a mong others, "What have you learned from reading this chapter?" "Wh at has remained in your memory after reading this chapter?" and "Wha t would you like to know more regarding the content of this chapter?" For the reading journal, the students were allowed to answer in Korea

n. Although the students could use vocabulary and phrases taken from the text for the summarization handout, this was not possible for the r eading journal because of its nature. Reflective journaling is about expre ssing subjective feelings; students were asked to write about what they were thinking while reading and how they felt. If they had been asked to write this in English, the reading journal would not hae been an act of reflection but rather an act of writing.

This handout was also turned in for teacher comments and returned du ring the Korean because the students had used Korean to write the refl ection. Table 5 presents an example of a student's reflection on a readi ng and subsequent teacher comments.

After completing the summarization and reading journal handouts, the students had group discussion only after the class had covered two reading chapter. As there were ten reading chapters, five group discussions took place. As a group, the students discussed and exchanged ideas freely about the two reading chapters they had covered. In order to prevent the students from misunderstanding each other as well as encourage them to express themselves in more detail, they were allowed to speak in Korean for this portion of the class, though all other class activities were performed in English. While the students shared their opinions and ideas in their small groups, the instructor visited each group listening to what was being said and giving advice. The instructor used English for the feedback. Even if the students asked questions in Korean, the instructor answered in English first. If the students could not understand the main point of the feedback, the instructor asked another group member to translate it in Korean. Only if the translation was incorrect or insufficient did the instructor use Korean to communicate.

Five individual writing sessions in total were held, one for every two re

Question	Student Answer
1.What do you remember the most from this chapter?	I was surprised that Leonardo da Vinci, Paul McCartney, and Julia Roberts are all left-handed because I like and respect them. Also, I remember that only 15% of the population in the world is left-handed.
Teacher Feedback	(no feedback provided)
2.What have you learned about the right brain?	The right brain controls the left side of the human body, and a right-handed person is usually punctual.
Teacher Feedback	*What other characteristics does a right-brained person have?*
3.What have you learned about the left brain?	The left brain controls the right side of the human body, and a left-handed person usually works with his hands, like an artist, writer, or inventor.
Teacher Feedback	*What other characteristics does a left-brained person have?*
4.What have you learned about yourself and your character?	I realized that I focused on only one side of the brain and did not use the other side.
Teacher Feedback	*Which side of the brain are you using? How does it affect your personality or character?*
5.What would you like to know more about after reading this chapter?	I wonder what kind of work a person who uses both the right and left brain could do and about his preferences.
Teacher Feedback	*What does the textbook say about both-handed users? What other things would you like to know outside of the textbook materials?*

Table 5

A Translated Example of Teacher Feedback on a Student's Reflection in His Reading Journal (Chapter 2: "My Character: Right Brain & Left Brain")

adings. After the group discussion, the instructor introduced one writing genre and three writing topics related to the reading. The students wrote one paragraph based on a given topic. Table 6 presents the textbook chapters and the related writing topics for the IRRF Group. Both the control and the RRF groups followed a different order of writing genres (Table 7). However, the topics assigned for each genre were the same for the three groups.

Reading Chapters	Genre of Writing	Given Topics
1 My Appearance 2 My Character	Opinion Paragraph	*The Best Feature of My Appearance for a Business Interview *The Best Part of My Character at Work *The Best Thing about Myself as a Worker
3 Character Change 4 A New Invention	Narrative Paragraph	(Business Interview) *A Story That Changed My Character *A Story of Creation in My Life *A Story of Changing a Habit
5 Another Invention 6 Creative Foods	Process Paragraph	*The Process of an Invention at Work *The Process of Making My Favorite Meal after Work *The Directions for Going to My Favorite Restaurant From School
7 Food History 8 History of Killer Bees	Descriptive Paragraph	(Business Interview) *A Description of the History of My Favorite Food *A Description of My Favorite Animal *A Description of My Favorite Thing
9 Another Danger 10 Dangerous Person	Example Paragraph	(Business Interview) *An Example of a Dangerous Event in My Life *An Example of a Dangerous Person Around Me *An Example of an Unexpected Event in My Daily Life

Table 6

Writing Types and Topics for Each Chapter: IRRF Group

Reading Chapters	Writing Type
Chapter 2 Chapter 1	Opinion Paragraph
Chapter 6 Chapter 5	Process Paragraph
Chapter 7 Chapter 4	Narrative Paragraph
Chapter 3 Chapter 10	Descriptive Paragraph
Chapter 9 Chapter 8	Example Paragraph

Table7

Writing Types for Each Chapter: Control and RRF Groups

An example outline was also provided to show the students how to w rite the paragraphs. Although the samples were presented as an outlin e, the students were asked to produce full paragraphs with complete sentences. The reasoning for this instructional design was that if the teacher provided a full-sentence sample; the students would be li kely to copy it. The outline was shown on the computer screen while t he students were composing in class. Table 8 present an example outlin e for an opinion paragraph. The other four genres varied in the details, but the general format was the same: an introduction, body, and concl usion.

Introduction	Stronger right brain
Body Topic 1	Emotional
Ex	Feeling affects studying final & friends fight
Body Topic 2	Love art
Ex	Museum to sooth my soul monthly basis
Conclusion	Topic 1 + 2: right brain better

Table 8
A Sample Outline for Paragraph Writing: Opinion Paragraph

In the next step, the students" paragraphs were collected, feedback was added by the teacher, and the writing was returned to the students. T he students were asked to revise their writing according to the commen ts, and the paragraphs were turned in once more. To ensure the studen ts made appropriate changes, the instructor checked the revised version side-by-side with the original. At this stage, a one-to-one conference bet ween the students and the instructor was provided to allow oral feedbac k and an opportunity to ask questions about their writing, further direc tions, and any comments that they could not clearly understand. The st udents could also share their ideas and opinions about their composition with the instructor. All three experiment groups received teacher feedba ck, as the writing and revision processes were not considered reflective s trategies.

The procedure of reading the text summarizing the main ideas, and co mpleting a reading journal followed by group discussion and an individ

Instructional Move	Control Group	RRF Group	IRRF Group
1 The first chapter reading	[Ch. 2] Practice comprehension questions: 1) Short answers' 2) Multiple choices 3) True or false	[Ch. 2] Practice reflective-reading strategies: 1) Summarization, 2) Reading journal, 3) Group discussion	[Ch. 1] Practice reflective-reading strategies: 1) Summarization, 2) Reading journal, 3) Group discussion
2 Grammar lecture (Ch. 1)	Practice handout and answer check		
3 The second chapter reading	[Ch. 1] Practice comprehension questions: 1) Short answers' 2) Multiple choices 3) True or false	[Ch. 1] Practice reflective-reading strategies: 1) Summarization, 2) Reading journal, 3) Group discussion	[Ch. 2] Practice reflective-reading strategies: 1) Summarization, 2) Reading journal, 3) Group discussion
4 Grammar lecture (Ch. 2)	Practice handout and answer check		
5 Student compose single paragraph writing	Opinion paragraph: Individual work		

Table 9

Instructional Procedures for the First Two Reading Chapters (One Iteration)

ual writing assignment was repeated five times in total for the ten cha pters with the two experimental groups. The control group, on the oth er hand, did not employ the three reflective strategies. Instead, as ment ioned earlier, the control group answered the comprehension questions i n the textbook after reading each chapter and moved directly to the si ngle paragraph writing practice (Table 9).

3.4.3 Instructional Procedure for the Sixteenth Week

To examine the potential changes in the students" writing proficiency, t he three following assessments were made at the end of the semester: p ost-test, retrospective composing-process survey, and self-reported of confi dence. Because this study examined the changes in the students" writin g proficiency, the awareness of their writing, and their confidence in wr

Stage	Description	Purpose
1	post-writing test	to examine the changes in the students' writing proficiency
2	retrospective composing-process survey	to assess the changes in the students' awareness about English composition
3	self-reported confidence in English writing	to assess changes in students' confidence in English writing

Table 10

Assessments at the End of the Semester

iting, the post-test used the same format as the pretest, but with differ ent questions. The retrospective composing-process survey and the self-co nfidence questions examined whether the students felt more confident in the writing process after one semester of reading-based writing instructio n incorporated intertextual and reflective-reading strategies with teacher feedback (IRRF). Table 10 provides further detail on the assessments.

3.5 Writing Measures

3.5.1 Scoring

The pre- and post-tests were scored by the researcher and a native spea ker of English (NSE) university instructor. The NSE instructor worked a t the university where the study was conducted and held a master"s de gree in English education from a U.S. university. The two evaluators met before the start of grading and read together preand post-test writings fr om an example student (These writings were not used in the data for th is study). They practiced twice and discussed the grading criteria while g oing over the scoring rubrics together; the correlation between the scores for the students" writings is included in the following results chapter. Each pre- and post-test was worth a possible 100 points (see Appendix

J for the scoring rubric). This was a combination of the two evaluators" grading. For example, pre-test question 1 (objective writing) and questio n 2 (subjective writing) were each worth up to 25 points, meaning the pre-test score from each evaluator was a maximum of 50 points. The p ost-test scored in the same way.

3.5.2 Writing Rubric

The scoring rubric used in this study was modified from Heaton (198 8). The original version evaluated five components of writing: content, organization, grammar, vocabulary, and punctuation. These components are identical to those used in the retrospective composing-process surve y, and students were encouraged to consider these factors on which thei r written work would be evaluated. The modified version of the rubric included the description reflecting the specific content and aims of the present study (see Appendix K).

Content was examined in terms of whether there was clear-connection b etween the assigned writing topics and what the students had actually written whether topic had been developed sufficiently. Because each cha pter was designed to enhance English-language skills for use in the busi ness field, the topic for the objective writing section of the pre-test was expected to be recognized as a business interview. If the students chose to interpret the picture differently, their score for content was low. Simi larly, the topic for the objective writing section of the post-test was a business trip. Writing about a personal trip or waiting for luggage in g eneral, for example, was not considered to be an appropriate topic.

Organization was evaluated in terms of whether the overall paragraph was coherent and whether there was cohesion between the individual sentences. The instructor provided a sample outline depicting typical paragraph organ ization (see Table 8 above) for students to use while writing the five diffe

rent genres of paragraph in class. This outline comprised an introduction, t

wo main ideas with supporting examples in the body, and a conclusion. In

order to prevent the students from copying example sentence structures, co

mplete sentences were not provided in the example.

The students'' paragraphs were examined in terms of the completeness of

sentences, correctness of sentence order, and accuracy in grammar. The

instructor gave ten grammar lectures in total during the experimental

period (Table 11). The grammar book used in the experiment was

assigned by the school where the study was conducted. After reading each

chapter, a lecture in PowerPoint on grammar was given to students (see

Appendix L for a sample of the PPT). A handout for practicing the

target chapter was also provided (see Appendix M). After the students

completed it, students volunteered to come to the board and write their

answers after which the instructor then went through each sentence with

the students. This process was repeated for the other nine chapters. The

scoring of grammar in the pre- and post-tests depended on the use of the

grammar acquired from these ten chapters. In particular, the instructor

taught students to produce complete sentences with appropriate subjects and

verbs for each writing assignment in class (i.e., to avoid fragments).

Although they learned about articles in Chapter 3 of the grammar book,

it was excluded from evaluation because these are difficult for non-native

speakers to use and the students had low proficiency in English. As the

last chapter of the grammar book focused on punctuation, only the first

nine chapters were used in the grading process for grammar.

The students' paragraphs were examined in terms of the appropriateness

of vocabulary choices and the variety of words used. Each chapter of the

textbook came with a glossary, and the students were expected to study

this to improve their vocabulary. After studying each chapter, students

Chapter	Grammar Focus
1	Present Tense: Simple vs. Present Continuous
2	Simple Past vs. Present Perfect
3	Articles
4	Sentence Patterns: Simple Sentences and Compound Sentences
5	Noun Clauses and Adjective Clauses
6	Adverbial Clauses
7	If Clauses and Verbs
8	Gerund vs. Infinitives
9	Passive
10	Punctuation and Capitalization

Table 11

The Grammar Chapters in the Grammar Book Used in the Study

were quizzed on the target vocabulary. Using the projector, the instructor typed the meaning of each word in Korean onto the computer screen for the students to see. The students were then asked to write the English word that best represented the meaning. If they could not remember the word used in the textbook, they were allowed to use a synonym. The

No.	Vocabulary
1	Have in common
2	Know what to do with
3	How intelligent
4	Rest of your life
5	Punctual
6	Have things in order
7	Plan things ahead
8	Practical
9	Logic, logical
10	At the same time
11	Recognize
12	Message

Table 12

A Glossary Sample: My Character (Chapter 2)

vocabulary quiz consisted of four questions for each chapter. The post-test evaluation for this component of writing depended on the extent to which the students used the learned vocabulary appropriately. A sample of the glossary from the Chapter 2 reading is presented in Table 12.

Categories	Content
A	How to use commas
B	How to use semicolons
C	How to use colons
D	Apostrophes
E	Periods
F	Rule for capitalization

Table 13

Sub-Categories of Punctuation in Chapter 10 of the Grammar Book Used in the Study

The punctuation score was based on appropriateness of the punctuation. The subcategories presented in the last chapter of the grammar book are listed in Table 13. If the students applied all of the sub-categories correc tly, they earned the maximum score. If they misused any of these punct uation types, each error cost on average -0.5 points.

3.6 Data Sets and Analysis

This study aimed to examine the effects of IRRF reading-based writing instruction on students" writing development. One control group and t wo experimental groups participated in the study. The following two tr eatments were combined: 1) intertextuality in reading and 2)reflective-re ading strategies with teacher feedback. The data were analyzed using on e-way ANCOVA, one-way ANOVA, and paired t-tests.

CHAPTER IV

RESULTS

This chapter presents the results of the data analysis of the present stu dy. The datacollected from the writing performance tests, the retrospect-composing process surveys, and the measurements of self-confidence refle ct the participants' writing proficiency, self-awareness, and self-confidence in English writing, respectively, at the time the study was conducted. The results of the overall writing test will be discussed first followed by the presentation of the results of objective and subjective types of writi ng test, writing awareness, and writing confidence.

4.1 One-Way ANOVA on Students' TOEIC Scores before th e Experiment

Beofore the experiment begins, the studnes wrote their TOEIC scores o n the survey if they had one. Table 14 and Figure 4 present the descri ptive statistics for the three groups' TOEIC scores.

A one-way ANOVA on the difference in the TOEIC scores of the thre e groups was performed. As can be seen in Table 15, the mean of the three groups was not significant (F (2, 99) = 2.36, p = .100). Theref ore, there was no difference in the students' proficiency levels before the experiment.

Group	N	Pre	
		Mean	SD
Control	35	481.57	136.47
RRF	32	397.97	127.14
IRRF	35	471.43	226.64

Table 14

Descriptive Data for Pre-TOEIC Scores

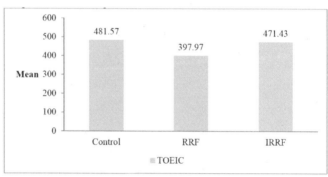

Figure 4

Comparison between Groups: Pre-TOEIC Scores

	Sum of Squares	df	Mean Square	F	p
Between Groups	137235.97	2	68617.98	2.36	.100
Within Groups	2880760.11	99	29098.59		

Note: *p<.05 **p<.01 ***p<.001   Dependent Variable: Pre-TOEIC Score

Table 15

One-Way ANOVA: Pre-TOEIC Scores

4.2 Quantitative Findings

4.2.1 One-Way ANCOVA on the Overall Writing Performance

The first research question was whether the IRRF reading-based writing instruction influences the scores of Korean EFL college students" writing performance. A one-way ANCOVA was performed to examine the differ ences between the three groups in the pre- and post-tests. Table 16 pr esents the descriptive statistics for the three groups.

Group	N	Pre		Post		Corrected Post	
		Mean	SD	Mean	SD	Mean	SE
Control	35	55.10	23.43	65.46	17.29	64.81	1.48
RRF	32	53.64	26.95	72.53	12.24	72.55	1.54
IRRF	35	52.29	25.70	77.45	13.13	78.08	1.48

Table 16
Descriptive Statistics for Pre, Post, and Corrected Post-Test Overall
Writing Scores

As can be seen in Table 16 and Figure 5, the pre-test mean scores for th e three groups were similar. However, after the experiment, the three grou

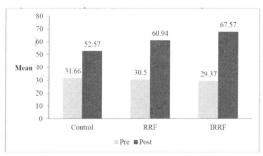

Figure 5
Comparison between Groups for Overall Pre- and
Post-Test Writing Scores

ps differed significantly, with the mean of the control group increasing fro
m 55.10 to 65.46, that of the RRF group increasing from 53.64 to 72.5
3, and that of the IRRF group increasing from 52.29 to 77.45

	Sum of Squares	df	Mean Square	F	p	Partial Eta Squared
Covariate (TOEIC)	475.71	1	475.71	5.52	.021*	.053
Group	3867.92	2	1933.96	22.46	.000***	.314
Error	8439.31	98	86.12			
Total	384281.00	102				

Note: *p<.05 **p<.01 ***p<.001   Dependent Variable: Post-Test Overal

Table 17

One-Way ANCOVA: Post-Test (Overall Scores)

A one-way ANCOVA was performed on the means of the post-test ove
rall scores for the three groups. As can be seen in Table 17, the differ
ence in the means of the three groups was statistically significant (F (2,
98) = 22.46, p < .001).

As shown in Table 18, post hoc tests (with Bonferroni correction) indicat
ed that the differences in means between the three groups were all signif
icant. The difference in means between the control and RRF groups was
-7.29 (p < .01), between control and IRRF groups was -14.87 (p < .00
1), and between RRF and IRRF groups was 7.58 (p < .05).

Group			Mean Difference	SD Error	p
Control	vs	RRF	-7.29	2.32	.007**
Control	vs	IRRF	-14.87	2.22	.000***
RRF	vs	IRRF	-7.58	2.31	.004**

Note: *p<.05 **p<.01 ***p<.001   Dependent Variable: Post-Test Overall

Table 18

Pairwise Comparison: Bonferroni (Post-Test Overall)

4.2.2 One-Way ANOVA on the Objective Writing and One-Way ANCOVA on the Subjective Writing

The second research question queried the effectiveness of IRRF reading-based writing instruction on objective and subjective writing. Table 19 presents the descriptive statistics for the three groups' objective writing test scores.

As can be seen in Table 19 and Figure 6, the pre-test objective writing scores for the three groups were similar before the experiment. However, after the experiment, these scores differed noticeably: the mean objective writing score increased from 16.49 to 26.23 for the control group, 15.88 to 28.81 for the RRF group, and from 13.51 to 32.26 for the IRRF group.

Group	N	Pre		Post	
		Mean	SD	Mean	SD
Control	35	16.49	7.62	26.23	6.41
RRF	32	15.88	6.39	28.81	3.87
IRRF	35	13.51	5.49	32.26	4.80

Table 19

Descriptive Data for the Pre and Post-Test Objective Writing Scores

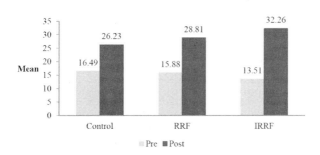

Figure 6

Comparison between Groups: Pre- and Post-Test Objective Writing

A one-way ANOVA on the difference in the post-test objective writing scores of the three groups was performed. As can be seen in Table 20, the means of the three groups were statistically different (F (2, 99) = 11.97, p < .001).

	Sum of Squares	df	Mean Square	F	p
Between Groups	640.08	2	320.04	11.97	.000***
Within Groups	2647.73	99	26.75		

Note: *p<.05 **p<.01 ***p<.001   Dependent Variable: Post-Test Objectiv·

Table 20

One-Way ANOVA: Post-Test Objective Writing Scores

Group			Mean Difference	SD Error	p
Control	vs	RRF	-2.58	1.26	.107
Control	vs	IRRF	-6.03	1.24	.000***
RRF	vs	IRRF	-3.44	1.26	.021*

Note: *p<.05 **p<.01 ***p<.001   Dependent Variable: Post-Test Objective

Table 21

Pairwise Comparison: Tukey HSD (Post-Test Objective Writing Scores)

As shown in Table 21, post hoc tests (Tukey HSD) indicated that the difference in means between the control and IRRF groups (-6.03; p < .0 01), and between the RRF and IRRF groups (-3.44; p < .05) were both statistically significant. However, the difference in means between the cont rol and RRF groups (-2.58; p = .107) was not statistically significant.

Table 22 and Figure 7 show the descriptive statistics for the three grou ps' subjective writing test scores. The pre-test subjective writing scores f or the three groups were similar before the experiment, but, the three g roups exhibited clear differences after; the mean subjective writing score increased from 15.17 to 26.34 for the control group, from 14.63 to 32. 13 for the RRF group, and from 15.86 to 35.31 for the IRRF group.

Group	N	Pre		Post		Corrected Post	
		Mean	SD	Mean	SD	Mean	SE
Control	35	15.17	6.01	26.34	7.10	26.36	.91
RRF	32	14.63	7.01	32.13	3.85	32.29	.96
IRRF	35	15.86	7.47	35.31	5.50	35.15	.92

Table 22

Descriptive Data for Pre, Post, and Corrected Post-Test Subjective
Writing Scores

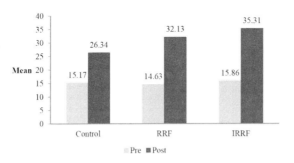

Figure 7

Comparison between Groups: Pre- and Post-Test Subjective
Writing

A one-way ANCOVA was performed on the mean scores for the post-test subjective writings of the three groups (Table 23), and they were found to be significantly different (F (2, 98) = 22.63, p < .001).

	Sum of Squares	df	Mean Square	F	p	Partial Eta Squared
Covariate (TOEIC)	195.25	1	195.25	6.36	.013*	.061
Group	1389.28	2	694.64	22.63	.000***	.316
Error	3007.68	98	30.69			
Total	104164.00	102				

Note: *p<.05 **p<.01 ***p<.001   Dependent Variable: Post-Test Subjective

Table 23

One-Way ANCOVA: Post-Test Subjective Writing Scores

As reported in Table 24, post hoc tests (with Bonferroni correction) found that the difference in means between the control and RRF groups (-5.09; p < .01), between the control and IRRF groups (-8.89; p < .001), and between the RRF and IRRF groups(-3.79; p < .05) were statistically significant.

Group			Mean Difference	SD Error	p
Control	vs	RRF	-5.09	1.38	.001**
Control	vs	IRRF	-8.89	1.33	.000***
RRF	vs	IRRF	-3.79	1.38	.021*

Note: *p<.05 **p<.01 ***p<.001   Dependent Variable: Post-Test Subjective

Table 24

Pairwise Comparison: Bonferroni (Post-Test Subjective Writing Scores)

4.2.3 One-Way ANOVA, One-Way ANCOVA, and t-Tests on the Five Components of Writing Evaluation

The third research objective was to establish which component of writing was most improved by IRRF reading-based writing instruction: content, organization, grammar, vocabulary, or punctuation.

A one-way ANOVA was performed to examine differences in content scores (maximum possible scores of 20) for the groups in the pre- and post- tests. Table 25 presents the descriptive statistics of the three groups. The pre-test mean content scores for the three groups were relatively low. However, after the experiment, the mean content score for all three groups rose dramatically, but this increase was much more noticeable in the two experimental groups; the mean of the control group increased from 7.94 to 11.09, that of the RRF group from 6.19 to 13.69, and that of the IRRF group from 5.89 to 14.40.

Group	N	Pre Mean	Pre SD	Post Mean	Post SD
Control	35	7.94	2.82	11.09	2.95
RRF	32	6.19	1.91	13.69	1.99
IRRF	35	5.89	2.31	14.40	2.02

Table 25

Descriptive Data for Pre and Post-Test Content Scores

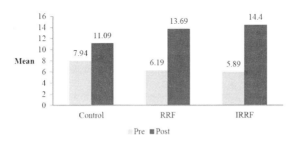

Figure 8

Comparison between Groups: Pre- and Post-Test Content Scores

A one-way ANOVA on the difference in means for the post-test content scores of the three groups was then performed, and the three groups were found to be significantly different (F (2, 99) = 18.79, p <.001).

	Sum of Squares	df	Mean Square	F	p
Between Groups	211.83	2	105.91	18.79	.000***
Within Groups	558.02	99	5.64		

Note: *p<.05 **p<.01 ***p<.001   Dependent Variable: Post-Test Content

Table 26

One-Way ANOVA: Post-Test Content Scores

Post hoc tests (Tukey HSD) found that the difference between the cont
rol and RRF groups in mean content scores was -2.60, and that betwee
n the control and IRRF groups was -3.31, both of which were statistica
lly significant (p <.001; Table 27).

However, the difference in means between the RRF and IRRF groups
(-.71; p = .440) did not reach statistical significance.

Group			Mean Difference	SD Error	p
Control	vs	RRF	-2.60	.58	.000***
Control	vs	IRRF	-3.31	.57	.000***
RRF	vs	IRRF	-.71	.58	.440

Note: *p<.05 **p<.01 ***p<.001   Dependent Variable: Post-Test Content

Table 27

Pairwise Comparison: Tukey HSD (Post-Test Content Scores)

A One-way ANOVA was performed to examine the differences in orga
nization scores (maximum score of 20) between the groups in the pre-
and post-tests. Table 28 presents the descriptive statistics of the three g
roups.

Group	N	Pre		Post	
		Mean	SD	Mean	SD
Control	35	7.34	3.01	10.60	3.16
RRF	32	6.19	1.98	13.19	1.87
IRRF	35	5.66	2.41	14.40	1.99

Table 28

Descriptive Data for Pre and Post-Test Organization Scores

As can be seen in Table 28 and Figure 9, the mean organization scores fo
r all three groups increased sharply between the pre- and post-test: from

7.34 to 10.60 for the control group, from 6.19 to 13.19 for the RRF gro up, and from 5.66 to 14.40 for the IRRF group. It can be seen that the mean organization scores for the two experimental groups demonstrated a greater increase than the mean score for the control group.

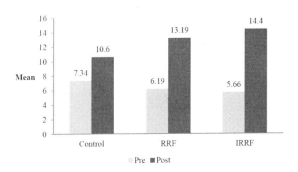

Figure 9

Comparison between Groups: Pre- and Post-Test Organization Scores

	Sum of Squares	df	Mean Square	F	p
Between Groups	263.08	2	131.54	22.39	.000***
Within Groups	581.68	99	5.88		

Note: *p<.05 **p<.01 ***p<.001   Dependent Variable: Post-Test Organization

Table 29

One-Way ANOVA: Post-Test Organization Scores

A one-way ANOVA on the mean organization scores for the post-test between the three groups was performed. As can be seen in Table 29, the difference in post-test means was statistically significant (F (2, 99) = 22.39, p < .001) between the three groups.

Group			Mean Difference	SD Error	p
Control	vs	RRF	-2.59	.59	.000***
Control	vs	IRRF	-3.80	.58	.000***
RRF	vs	IRRF	-1.21	.59	.107

Note: *p<.05 **p<.01 ***p<.001　　Dependent Variable: Post-Test Organization

Table 30

Pairwise Comparison: Tukey HSD (Post-Test Organization Scores)

As reported in Table 30, post hoc tests (Tukey HSD) found a significant difference in the organization scores of the control and RRF groups (-2.59; p < .001), and of the control and IRRF groups (-3.80; p < .001). The means of the RRF and IRRF groups were not statistically significant (-1.21, p = .107).

A one-way ANCOVA was performed to examine the differences in grammar score (maximum score of 20) between the groups in the pre- and post-test. Table 31presents the descriptive statistics for the three groups. The mean grammar scores increased noticeable for all three groups between the pre-test (control = 6.57; RRF = 6.19; IRRF = 5.03) and the post-test (control = 9.31; RRF = 13.19; IRRF = 12.09), with the two experimental groups showing the greatest improvement.

Group	N	Pre		Post		Corrected Post	
		Mean	SD	Mean	SD	Mean	SE
Control	35	6.57	2.91	9.31	2.08	9.20	.30
RRF	32	6.19	1.98	13.19	1.87	10.79	.31
IRRF	35	5.03	2.26	12.09	1.95	12.22	.30

Table 31

Descriptive Data for Pre, Post, and Corrected Post-Test Grammar Scores

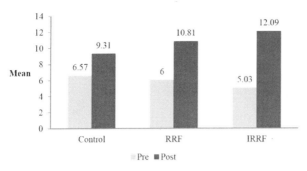

Figure 10

Comparison between Groups: Pre- and Post-Test Grammar Scores

A one-way ANCOVA was subsequently performed on the difference in mean grammar score in the post-test for the three groups (Table 32); it was found that the post-test grammar scores were significantly different (F (2, 98) = 21.51, p < .001).

	Sum of Squares	df	Mean Square	F	p	Partial Eta Squared
Covariate (TOEIC)	16.12	1	16.12	5.25	.024*	.051
Group	132.17	2	66.09	21.51	.000***	.305
Error	301.04	98	3.07			
Total	12207.00	102				

Table 32

One-Way ANCOVA: Post-Test Grammar Scores

Group			Mean Difference	SD Error	p
Control	vs	RRF	-1.30	.44	.011*
Control	vs	IRRF	-2.75	.42	.000***
RRF	vs	IRRF	-1.45	.44	.004**

Note: *p<.05 **p<.01 ***p<.001   Dependent Variable: Post-Test Grammar

Table 33

Pairwise Comparison: Bonferroni (Post-Test Grammar Scores)

The mean difference in mean grammar score for each pairing among th e three groups was statistically significant as confirmed by post hoc test s with Bonferroni correction (Table 33). The mean difference between c ontrol and RRF groups was -1.30(p < .05), that between the control a nd IRRF groups was -2.75 (p < .001), and that between the RRF and IRRF groups was -1.45 (p < .01).

A one-way ANOVA was performed to examine the differences in vocab ulary scores among the groups in the pre- and post-tests. Table 34 pre sents the descriptive statistics for the three groups.

Group	N	Pre		Post	
		Mean	SD	Mean	SD
Control	35	7.11	2.72	10.54	2.41
RRF	32	6.13	2.96	11.13	1.07
IRRF	35	5.31	2.49	12.77	2.06

Table 34

Descriptive Data for Pre and Post-Test Vocabulary Scores

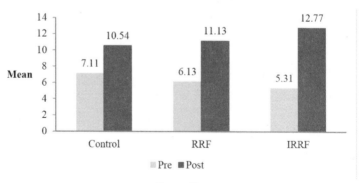

Figure 11

Comparison between Groups: Pre- and Post-Test Vocabulary Scores

As for the previous three components, there was a clear increase in ave rage scores for vocabulary in all three groups between the pre- and pos t-test, with the two experimental groups showing the most dramatic inc rease: the RRF group from 6.31 to 11.13, and the IRRF group from 5.31 to 12.77 (Table 34; Figure 11).

A one-way ANOVA on the mean vocabulary scores in the post-test for the three groups was performed; as can be seen in Table 35, the mean s the three groups were significantly different (F (2, 99) = 12.25, p < .001).

	Sum of Squares	df	Mean Square	F	p
Between Groups	93.13	2	46.57	12.25	.000***
Within Groups	376.36	99	3.80		

Note: *p<.05 **p<.01 ***p<.001   Dependent Variable: Post-Test Vocabulary

Table 35

One-Way ANOVA: Post-Test Vocabulary

Group			Mean Difference	SD Error	p
Control	vs	RRF	-.58	.48	.444
Control	vs	IRRF	-2.23	.47	.000***
RRF	vs	IRRF	-1.65	.48	.002**

Note: *p<.05 **p<.01 ***p<.001   Dependent Variable: Post-Test Vocabulary

Table 36

Pairwise Comparison: Tukey HSD (Post-Test Vocabulary)

Subsequent post hoc tests (Tukey HSD) found a significant difference in mean vocabulary scores between the control and RRF groups (-.2.23; p < .001), and between the RRF and IRRF groups (-1.65; p < .01). Ho wever, the mean difference between the control and RRF groups (-.58; p = .444) did not reach statistical significance (Table 36).

A one-way ANCOVA was performed to examine the differences in mean punctuation scores (maximum score of 20) between the experimental groups in the pre-and post-tests. Table 37 presents the descriptive statistics for the three groups.

Group	N	Pre		Post		Corrected Post	
		Mean	SD	Mean	SD	Mean	SE
Control	35	7.26	2.74	11.11	2.73	10.97	.37
RRF	32	5.81	2.88	12.06	1.50	12.36	.40
IRRF	35	7.17	2.76	13.80	2.55	13.68	.37

Table 37

Descriptive Data for Pre, Post, and Corrected Post-Test Punctuation Scores

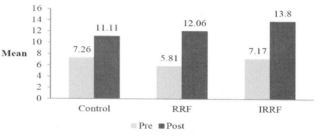

Figure 12

Comparison between Groups: Pre- and Post-Test Punctuation

As can be seen in Table 37 and Figure 12, and following a similar trend to the previous assessed components of writing, punctuation scores increased between the pre-test and post-test for all three groups, with the two experimental groups exhibiting a larger improvement (RRF, pre-M = 5.81, post-M = 12.06; IRRF pre-M = 7.17, post-M = 13.80) than the control group (pre-M = 7.26, post-M = 11.11).

The one-way ANCOVA, summarized in Table 38, found that the mean vocabulary scores for the three groups in the post-test differed significantly (F (2, 98) =12.69, p < .001).

	Sum of Squares	df	Mean Square	F	p	Partial Eta Squared
Covariate (TOEIC)	33.52	1	33.52	6.42	.013*	.062
Group	132.49	2	66.24	12.69	.000***	.206
Error	511.49	98	5.22			
Total	16190.00	102				

Note: *p<.05 **p<.01 ***p<.001   Dependent Variable: Post-Test Punctuation

Table 38

One-Way ANCOVA: Post-Test Punctuation

Group			Mean Difference	SD Error	p
Control	vs	RRF	-.66	.57	.743
Control	vs	IRRF	-2.65	.55	.000***
RRF	vs	IRRF	-1.99	.57	.002**

Note: *p<.05 **p<.01 ***p<.001   Dependent Variable: Post-Test Punctuation

Table 39

Pairwise Comparison: Bonferroni (Post-Test Punctuation)

The post hoc tests (with Bonferroni correction, summarized in Table 39) uncovered a statistically significant difference in mean punctuation scores between the control and IRRF groups (-2.65; p < .001), and between t he RRF and IRRF groups (-1.99; p < .01). However, there was no signi ficant difference between the control and RRF groups (-.66, p = .743).

t-Test. A paired sample t-test was performed on the IRRF group for ea ch assessed component of writing, and the overall comparison within th e five domains was also examined. Only the scores of the IRRF group were use as this was the only group that was exposed to the full range of intertextual and reflective-reading strategies with teacher feedback (IR RF). Table 40 shows the descriptive statistics for the five components.

Area	N	Pre Mean	Pre SD	Post Mean	Post SD	t	df	p
Content	35	5.98	2.31	14.40	2.02	-15.82	34	.000***
Organization	35	5.66	2.41	14.40	1.99	-15.11	34	.000***
Grammar	35	5.03	2.26	12.09	1.95	-14.66	34	.000***
Vocabulary	35	5.31	2.49	12.77	2.06	-14.41	34	.000***
Punctuation	35	7.17	2.76	13.80	2.55	-10.29	34	.000***

Note: * $p<.05$ ** $p<.01$ *** $p<.001$ Dependent Variable: Post Test Scores

Table 40

Paired t-Test for Five Components of Writing: IRRF Group

As can be seen in Table 40 and Figure 12, all five components of writ
ing exhibited a statistically significant increase in score between the pre-
and post-test. Content was the component most strongly improved by I
RRF reading-based writing instruction (preM = 5.98, postM = 14.40,
t = -15.82), followed by organization, grammar, vocabulary, and punct
uation.

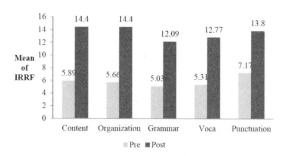

Figure 13

Comparison between the Five Assessed Writing Components:
Pre- and Post-Test

4.2.4 One-Way ANOVA on Students' Writing Awareness

The fourth research question was whether IRRF reading-based writing in struction increases the self-awareness of Korean EFL college students' wr iting performance. A one-way ANOVA was performed to examine whet her the differences in the retrospect-composing process survey before and after the experiment were statistically significant. Table 41 shows the de scriptive statistics for the three groups.

As can be seen in Table 41 and Figure 14, all three groups increased i n their self-awareness over the course of the study, with the IRRF grou p demonstrating the largest change (preM = 10.51, postM = 12.80).

Group	N	Pre		Post	
		Mean	SD	Mean	SD
Control	35	9.54	4.27	10.20	3.09
RRF	32	11.25	2.93	12.69	2.61
IRRF	35	10.51	2.87	12.80	2.71

Table 41
Descriptive Data for the Pre and Post-Survey
Self-Awareness

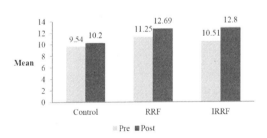

Figure 14
Comparison between Groups: Pre- and Post-Survey
Self-Awareness Scores

	Sum of Squares	df	Mean Square	F	p
Between Groups	149.27	2	74.63		
				9.40	.000***
Within Groups	786.08	99	7.94		

Note: *p<.05 **p<.01 ***p<.001   Dependent Variable: Post-Survey

Table 42

One-Way ANOVA: Post-Survey Self-Awareness

The one-way ANOVA on the mean difference in self-awareness as meas ured in the post-test found that three groups exhibited a statistically sig nificant difference in their self-awareness (F (2, 99) = 9.40, p < .001; Table 42).

Table 43 presents the result of post hoc tests (Tukey HSD) on the me an self- awareness differences between the three groups. Significant differ ences were found in mean self-awareness between the control and RRF groups (-2.49; p < .01), and between the control and IRRF groups (-2.60; p < .01), but the mean difference between the RRF and IRRF g roups was insignificant (-.11; p = .985).

Group			Mean Difference	SD Error	p
Control	vs	RRF	-2.49	.69	.001**
Control	vs	IRRF	-2.60	.67	.001**
RRF	vs	IRRF	-.11	.69	.985

Note: *p<.05 **p<.01 ***p<.001   Dependent Variable: Post-Survey

Table 43

Pairwise Comparison: Tukey HSD (Post-Survey Self-Awareness)

4.2.5 One-Way ANOVA on Students' Writing Confidence

The fifth research question was whether IRRF reading-based writing inst ruction increases the self-confidence of Korean EFL college students in t heir writing. A one-way ANOVA was performed to investigate this que stion. Table 44 shows the descriptive statistics for the three groups.

Group	N	Pre		Post	
		Mean	SD	Mean	SD
Control	35	1.03	.62	1.45	.80
RRF	32	1.13	.79	1.44	.80
IRRF	35	.89	.68	1.49	.61

Table 44
Descriptive Data for Pre and Post-Confidence Scores

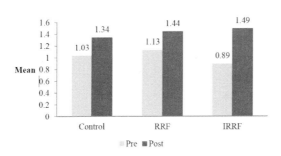

Figure 15
Comparison between Groups: Pre- and Post-Confidence

Table 44 and Figure 15 report that the three groups showed little diffe rence after the experiment in their mean self-confidence. The one-way A NOVA (Table 45)confirmed that the difference in mean post-confidence scores between the three groups was not significant (F (2, 99) = .34, p =.716). It should be noted, however, that the IRRF group had a no ticeably lower self-confidence before the experiment (M = .89)than did the control (M = 1.03) and RRF groups (M 1.13), yet by the end of the experiment, self-confidence in this group was very slightly higher th an the other two.

	Sum of Squares	df	Mean Square	F	p
Between Groups	.37	2	.18	.34	.716
Within Groups	54.50	99	.55		

Note: *p<.05 **p<.01 ***p<.001   Dependent Variable: Post-Confidence

Table 45

One-Way ANOVA: Post-Confidence

4.3 Pearson Correlations between Evaluators on the Writing Performance Test

In order to see the correlation between the two evaluators on the writi ng performance tests, Pearson correlations were computed (Table 46). T he Pearson correlation coefficients were. 95 for the pre-test and .92 for the post-test; statistically significant in both cases (p < .001). Given th at a correlation of at least. 6 or more is needed to be considered mean ingful (Sung, 2007), the degree of agreement between the two evaluato rs was deemed satisfactory.

Evaluator	N	Pre	Post	p
A	102	.95	.92	.000***
B	102	.95	.92	.000***

Note: *p<.05 **p<.01 ***p<.001

Table 46

Pearson Correlation: Pre and Post-Test

CHAPTER V

DISCUSSION

The purpose of the current study was to examine the effects of reading -based writing instruction that incorporated intertextual and reflective-rea ding strategies with teacher feedback (IRRF) on Korean EFL college learn ers' writing development. Intertextuality has been considered an important factor in the effective understanding of reading material, while reflective-r eading in conjunction with teacher feedback has been found to improve r eading and writing proficiency in a variety of educational setting, includin g L2 reading and writing in EFL (Beach, Appleman, & Dorsey, 1990; Bi ggs, 1999). However, the effectiveness of the two factors together in EFL reading-based writing instruction has yet to be investigated. This combine d model has the potential to be a new instructional strategy in EFL writ ing education. This study harnesses the close relationship between reading and writing, and applies reading knowledge to writing improvement, a pr ocess that would be especially useful from EFL at the college level.

5.1 Quantitative Research

By measuring the changes in pre- and post-writing test scores and focu sing on the effects of IRRF reading-based writing instruction on both o bjective and subjective writing, this study attempted to determine wheth er this form of instruction helped students to develop their writing prof

iciency. This study also examined five components of writing to establis
h which area, if any, benefitted the most from this instructional strateg
y. Finally, the change in writing awareness and confidence among the s
tudents over the 16-week experiment was measured with pre- and post-
experimental retrospective composing-process surveys.

5.1.1 The Effects of IRRF Reading-Based Writing Instruction on Overall Writing Performance

The first research question investigated the effect of the IRRF reading-b
ased writing instruction on EFL college learners' writing performance. T
he one-way ANCOVA for the post-test identified differences in the perf
ormance of the three groups. The RRF group scored higher in the writi
ng test than the control group, and the IRRF group performed better s
till. This suggests that IRRF reading-based writing instruction was effect
ive in its primary purpose of improving general writing proficiency. This
results in supported by previous research that found intertextuality and
reflective reading are helpful for reading comprehension and share a posi
tive relationship with writing development (Eckoff, 1993; Grabe, 2003).

5.1.2 The Effects of IRRF Reading-Based Writing Instruction on Objective and Subjective Writing

The present study then investigated which type of writing, objective or su
bjective, benefitted more from IRRF instruction by comparing the writing
scores from the pre-and post-tests for both types individually. Objective w
riting was categorized as being informational or descriptive in nature, whil
e subjective writing was categorized as stating an opinion or solving a pro
blem. According to McCarthey, Guo, and Cummins(2005), when writing i
s taught, the different types and genres of writing should beconsidered.

The one-way ANOVA for the post-test objective found that, of the two experimental groups, only the IRRF group performed better than the co ntrol group. This result provides support for the claim that reflective-re ading strategy instruction with teacher feedback should be accompanied by intertextuality in order to better develop objective writing. This resul t also supports the findings of previous research, for example, Hartman' s (1995) study on the use of intertextuality for more meaningful interac tion between the reader and text reported that building an intertextual connection helps learners to improve linguistic ability, making it easier t o transfer knowledge from reading to writing.

The one-way ANCOVA for the post-test subjective writing identified dif ferences in the performance of the three groups. The RRF group scored hi gher in the writing test than the control group, and the IRRF group perf ormed better still. This suggests that IRRF reading-based writing instructio n was effective in its primary purpose of improving general writing proficie ncy. This results in supported by previous research hat found intertextualit y and reflective reading are helpful for reading comprehension and share a positive relationship with writing development (Eckoff, 1993; Grabe, 2003). The finding that reflective-reading with teacher feedback (RRF) was still important for subjective writing, while intertextuality was only beneficial for objective writing can be explained by the characteristics of the reflec tive-reading method. Because it is a subjective process of learning, invol ving the review of class material and looking back on personal experien ces, students are likely to approach the subsequent writing from a varie ty of individual perspectives depending on each student's ability, persona l history, and current situation in life (Brookfield & Brookfield, 1995). I n other words, their internalization of class material is likely to differ d epending on how well each student understands certain units or topics. Therefore, subjective writing may be more directly related to reflective-r eading than objective writing is, and intertextuality is unlikely to make a difference. While subjective writing performance can improve without the introduction of intertextuality, objective writing may require it in or der to more effectively transfer reading knowledge to writing.

5.1.3 The Effects of IRRF Reading-Based Writing Instruction on the Five Components of Writing

The third research question focused on which component of writing, if an y, was most improved by IRRF reading-based writing instruction. For the content and organization scores in the post-test writing, the RRF group pe rformed significantly better than the control group; however, there was no significant difference between the two experimental groups. In other words, reflective-reading strategies with teacher feedback (RRF) was found to be more effective than traditional instruction for these two components of writ ing, and the presence of intertextuality did not have a noticeable effect.

For this writing component, both experimental groups demonstrated signi ficantly higher scores in the post-test than the control group did. It was also found that the IRRF group performed better than the RRF group. Therefore, it can be assumed that, in this study at least, IRRF reading-b ased writing instruction was effective in improving written grammar.

Of the two experimental groups, only the IRRF group had a statisticall y higher mean score than the control group in the post test. This resul t suggests that intertextuality may play an important role in vocabulary building and in the learning of spelling.

The t-test results showed that the scores for all five assessed writing co mponents increased significantly between the pre- and post-test. This is supported by the findings of Caudery (1998) demonstrated that reading-based writing instruction is effective for writing development. The prese nt study also reinforce the benefits of intertextuality and reflective readi ng outlined by Chi (1998) and Zeichner (1994), and support Jones and

Jones' (2013) conjecture that reading can lead to more effective writing under the skilled guidance of a teacher.

Of the five components assessed in this study, content experienced the s trongest positive effect for the experimental instruction, and punctuation the smallest. Although the t-values did not differ greatly across the five components, the higher value for content suggested that is benefitted m ost from the experimental instruction in this study.

One possible reason for this outcome could be students' consideration of the order of the assessed items. Since content was the first aspect of th eir writing evaluated on the rubric, students might have thought that it was the most important. Another possibility is that content (and organiz ation, which had the second largest t-statistic) may be able to be learne d faster with the teacher's explanation than the other components. Becau se the expectations for the content were clearly communicated and a sa mple outline was presented before each of the in-class writings, content and organization may have been easier for the students to improve on.

In contrast, 16 weeks (the length of the semester) may not been long enough to dramatically improve grammar or vocabulary. Students were provided with a list of essential vocabulary words and phrases for each chapter and given grammar correction for each piece of writing they pr oduced, but they tended to practice and memorize these particular word s only and little else. In the pre- and post-tests, students were recomm ended to use other words in addition to those from the texts, but unle ss they studied grammar and vocabulary outside of class, which did not seem to happen, these two areas could not be as easily improved as co ntent and organization.

Punctuation showed the least improvement of the five components of w riting evaluated. Although students were marked for incorrect spelling a nd punctuation use in their writing, and asked to be mindful of these i n the rewriting process, they did not seem to consider punctuation as i mportant as the other areas. Students knew that they had to spell corr ectly in English but in the pre- and post-tests, many of them forgot to put periods or question marks at the ends of sentences. This showed th at they were not familiar with written punctuation in English.

5.1.4 The Effects of IRRF Reading-Based Writing Instruction on Students' Writing Awareness

This study used a retrospective composing-process survey to examine the difference, if any, between the students' writing awareness before and afte r the experiment, which was the subject of the fourth research question. The questions in the survey required the students to assess their awarenes s of the same five components used as regarding criteria for the pre- and post-writing tests: content, organization, grammar, vocabulary, and punctu ation. Students were encouraged to think about these areas while writing Reading-based writing helps learners to engage in a deep thinking proces s during the writing process, and as such, the students in the present st udy were able to develop and enhance their awareness of what to write and how to write it (Ede & Lunsford, 1990; Flahive & Bailey, 1993).

The one-way ANOVA for the post experimental survey found that the RRF group had a higher awareness of the individual components of thei r writing than the control group did; there was no difference between t he two experimental groups in this aspect. These findings suggest that reflective-reading with teacher feedback (RRF) was more effective than t raditional instruction in creating awareness of the writing process in the students, and intertextuality was not an important factor in this case.

Reflective-reading and teacher feedback are both known to be advantage ous for learner awareness. For example, Day (1993) concluded that refle ctive-reading encourages learners to consider topics from different and br oader perspectives. The results of the present study also support Miao

(2006), who asserted that EFL students with low-level reading and writing skills are not able to find their own mistakes; therefore, appropriate teacher feedback helps them to develop a more effective cognitive approach to brainstorming in the learning process.

5.1.5 The Effects of IRRF Reading-Based Writing Instruction on Students' Writing Confidence

In order to answer the fifth research question, the study investigated the self-reported scores of students' writing confidence. It was found that there were no differences between the three groups in their post-experiment confidence, though all three groups increased in mean confidence score between the start and the end of the experiment. One reason for this conclusion could be the subjects of the present study. Most of them had never received writing instruction before they were placed in the experiment, thus many tended to have low self-esteem concerning their writing skills in English before the experiment started. It may be that any form of structured writing instruction had the power to improve self-confidence if delivered to these students in a supportive environment.

That said, IRRF reading-based writing instruction is still recommended as a way to improve EFL learners' writing confidence, for example, Liston and Zeichner (1990) demonstrated that intertextual reading raised confidence in the target language. It may be possible that, in the present study, 16 weeks of IRRF reading-based writing instruction was not long enough to increase students' self-confidence beyond that achievable by traditional instruction . However, this would require further empirical investigation.

CHAPTER VI

CONCLUSION AND IMPLICATIONS

6.1 Findings

The five objectives of the current study were to investigate the effects o f reading-based writing instruction that incorporated intertextual and refl ective-reading strategies with teacher feedback (IRRF) in an EFL setting on the following: 1) overall writing performance, 2) objective and subjec tive writing performance, 3) the five main components of writing (conte nt, organization, grammar, vocabulary, punctuation), 4) student self-awar eness of their writing process, and 5) student self-confidence in writing.

In terms of the first objective, IRRF reading-based writing instruction i mproved Korean EFL college students' overall writing performance. The results of the current study suggested that both forms of intertextuality (providing background information on a text and presenting a series of texts in a logical order) applied together in reading had a positive effec t on writing development. It also indicated that the students used reflec tive-reading strategies to reflect on and review class materials in conjunc tion while looking back on personal experiences in order to make conne ctions to the chapter being studied. Students were encouraged to do bo th of these things when they wrote in their journals, which seemed to help improve their writing.

Second, the students' writing improved in both objective and subjective types under the reading-based writing instruction. In this study, the objective writing test asked the students to describe a scene in a photo, and the subjective writing test was asked them to take one side of a controversial issue. Although IRRF instruction was useful for both types of writing, objective writing benefitted more from intertextuality than subjective writing did.

Third, the students' writing improved in the five components under the reading-based writing instruction, though vocabulary and punctuation appeared to benefit more from intertextuality than did content, organization, and grammar.

Content and organization improved slightly more than grammar, vocabulary, and punctuation. It is probable that content and organization were easier for students to improve than were grammar, vocabulary, and punctuation, all of which may have needed targeted instruction for greater improvement to be shown.

Fourth, this study revealed that RRF reading-based writing instruction was effective in improving students' self-awareness of their writing process. It also suggested that intertextuality and reflective-reading with teacher feedback do not need to be applied together as far as writing awareness is concerned.

Fifth, the study investigated the effect of IRRF reading-based writing instruction on students' self-confidence in English writing. Although their confidence scores rose to a small extent, self-confidence was still relatively low at the end of the 16 week semester.

6.2 Pedagogical Implications of the Study

The current study was conducted to examine whether IRRF reading-base d writing instruction could enhance English writing performance in Kor ean college students. It investigated the effect of this instructional strate gy across the three groups: a control group, which followed the activitie s in the textbook assigned to the writing class, an experimental group t hat was exposed to reflective-reading strategies with teacher feedback (R RF), and a second experimental group that was exposed to reflective- re ading strategies with teacher feedback with the addition of intertexuality in the reading (IRRF). From the results of the study, some pedagogical implications for EFL reading-based writing classrooms can be drawn.

First, the study examined both objective and subjective writing separatel y. Writing classes often choose to focus on specific genres of writing, s uch as descriptive or argumentative, for the entire course, or for certain units within a course. For objective writing, such as describing an imag e or a situation, the results of the presen study suggest that intertextua lity should be used in classroom instruction along with reflective-reading and teacher feedback. Holmes (2004) reported that intertextuality was b eneficial to reading skills and resultant comprehension, which can then be transferred to writing. In contrast, in the teaching of subjective writi ng in the form of a genre like the opinion paragraph, reflective-reading with teacher feedback would appear to be sufficient, based on the result s of the present study. The addition of intertextual order, however, it c an bring about a stronger effect.

Second, in the examination of the five components of writing, this stud y suggests that, when teaching vocabulary and punctuation, intertextuali ty should be used along with reflective-reading strategies with teacher f eedback. In contrast, in the teaching of content and organization, reflective-reading and teacher feedback (RRF) should be treated as more important than considerations of intertextual order.

Third, it is recommended that teachers provide more opportunities to study grammar, vocabulary, and punctuation under IRRF reading-based writing instruction. Since most of the students in this study were unable (or unwilling) to study on their own outside of class, if the teacher had provided them with more than just word lists from the textbook, it would have helped them to develop a more diverse writing vocabulary. Activities such as having students search for and select grammar patterns and useful phrases from the reading texts themselves would help them to become familiar with correct (and commonly used) grammar forms. Reflective-reading is known to be a skill that promotes learner autonomy; therefore students should internalizing the new information, and connecting that to their writing (Alger, 2006). They also need to acknowledge the importance of proper punctuation in English writing, and the teacher can provide more practice for the learning of spelling.

Fourth, the instructional model of the current study is most effective when the readings are presented in intertextual order. However, in some colleges teachers may not be authorized to change the order of texts in lesson planning for administrative reasons. In these cases, they can still utilize reflective-reading strategies with teacher feedback without intertextuality, which was shown in this study to be more effective than traditional instruction, which also did not consider intertextual order. In fact, reflective-reading and teacher feedback are both well known to be helpful in developing reading skills and making connections to writing (Alger, 2006; Hyland &Hyland, 2001). In addition, first aspect of intertextuality ‑ providing background information on the text being read ‑ can still be corporate in a classroom with fixed reading lists. Additional backg round information is known from previous studies to help improve readi ng comprehension (Green & Meyer, 1991; Irwin, 2004; Lewis, 2008). Fifth, individual writing often lacks interest for learners who have little motivation to improve their English language and composition skills. Lo w-level EFL students, who are afraid of writing in the target language, usually feel more comfortable working together in pairs or as a group. Examining the impact of the IRRF reading-based writing instruction on EFL group writing would be another interesting study in the field of E nglish writing education.

6.3 Limitations and Suggestions for Future Research

There were a few limitations in the current study. First, the data obtai ned in this study was from one particular college in Korea, so replicati ng the study at different colleges would increase the generalizability of the results. Furthermore, the subjects of the study were all second-year students, and their individual characteristics and majors were not conside red. Even though the subjects were a representative sample of the stude nt population, there should be caution in making generalizations from t he study results.

In addition, writing performance was measured with modified TOEIC a nd TOEFL writing test questions. Other official writing tests and differe nt types of evaluations could lead to different results.

Also worth considering is the fact that, although self-confidence increase d under the IRRF reading-based writing instruction with teacher feedbac k, it was not statistically significant. One reason could be the short len gth of the experiment. If the study had been conducted over more tha n the 16 weeks, the results for self-confidence may have diverged furthe

r. Korean students learning English also have a tendency to look down on their own ability, so they may have rated themselves lower than what they were actually capable of. Another issue is that the students wrote their names on the top of the self-confidence survey and they may have worried about the teacher's opinion on their writing performance and their actual scores in comparison to the confidence they reported. For example, if they reported themselves as having high confidence but their final grade came out low, students might worry what the instructor thought of them. In addition, the subjects were non-English majors and most of them struggled in English. If they were English majors or selecting the course as an elective rather enrolling as a college graduation requirement, the results for self-confidence may have differed.

Another issue was that, because the students had relatively low proficiency, the five in-class writings were done as individual tasks. If the students were of a higher level and familiar with reflective-reading strategies, writing with peers in groups would have been an interesting research topic. However, because the pre- and post-tests were based on individual writing, it was necessary that the in-class writings follow the same standard.

The evaluation of grammar and vocabulary also ran into a possible limitation. On aim was for students to use the grammar and vocabulary learned in class in the post-test. However, because the students had relatively low proficiency levels; the evaluation was dominated by superficial errors in their writing such as errors in grammar or spelling, and thus it was difficult to accurately measure the actual degree of vocabulary and grammar learning that took place.

The following are suggested as avenues of further study. First, the study was done in an EGP course, and it would be informative to replicate the study in English for Specific Purpose (ESP) or English major classro oms. If the results are similar to those of the current study, it provides further support for the use of the IRRF reading-based writing instructio n model in composition classes.

Second, this model could also be introduced at different school levels, w ith studies at elementary, middle, and high schools, and with adults are encouraged. Analyzing the results from other levels of education would enable the developmental patterns in English writing to be traced.

Third, the used of IRRF reading-based writing instruction could also be investigated in different countries. The current study was conducted in Korea, but it has a cultural and educational context that differs from o ther Asian countries such as China or Japan. By expanding the model presented in the present study to the EFL tertiary level in other countri es, the suitability of the instructional model for international application could be assessed.

Fourth, the instructional model could also be studied within a group wr iting setting. The results could then be compared to those of this study to determine which setting is more effective in developing students' writ ing skills. Interviews with students asking if they feel more comfortable writing individually or in a group would also be helpful. Factors such a s major, level, grade, and gender should be taken into consideration wh en forming writing groups and analyzing the results.

Finally, vocabulary acquisition skills could be added to IRRF reading-bas ed writing instruction. After learning new vocabulary and understanding how it is used in natural communication, students may be able to used the vocabulary more effectively in their writing.

REFERENCES

Abasi, A. R., & Akbari, N. (2008). Are we encouraging patch writing? Reconsidering the role of the pedagogical context in ESL student writers'transgressive intertextuality. English for Specific Purposes, 2 7(3), 267-284.

Abrams, S. S., & Gerber, H. R. (2013). Achieving through the feedbac k loop:Videogames, authentic assessment, and meaningful learning. English Journal, 103(1), 95-103.

Agazade, A. S. & Vefali, G. M. (2013). Frequency versus importance: L anguage learning strategy use in the EFL classroom. Applied Lang uage Learning, 23(24), 47-62.

Ahn, D. H. (2001). The internet as an educational tool in English readin g and writing instruction for Korean college students. Language Sci ence, 8(2), 63-91.

Ahn, S. (2007). Comparison of achievement in step-up learning (Unpublis hed master's Thesis). Daejin University, Pocheon.

Akinbode, A. (2013). Teaching as lived experience: The value of explorin g the hidden and emotional side of teaching through reflective narr atives. Studying Teacher Education, 9(1), 62-73.

Alger, C. (2006). What went well, what didn't go so well: Growth of r eflection in pre-service teachers". Reflective Practice, 7(3), 287-301

Al-Hazmi, S., & Schofield, P. (2007). Enforced revision with checklist a
nd peer feedback in EFL writing. Scientific Journal of King Faisal
University, 8(2), 237-267.

Allen, G. (2011). Intertextuality (2nd ed.). New York: Routledge.

Anderson, L. M. (1992). Teaching writing with a new instructional mod
el: Variations in teacher"s beliefs, instructional practice, and their s
tudents" performance. East Lansing, MI: Michigan University Press.

Anrends, R. (1998). Learning to Teach. (4th ed.) New York: McGraw-Hill.

Anson, C. M. (2000). Reflective reading: Developing thoughtful ways to
respond to students" writing. In McDonald, J. (Ed.), Sourcebook f
or College Writing Teachers (pp. 374-393).. Boston, MA; Allyn a
nd Bacon.

Archer, J. M. (2001). Old Worlds: Egypt, Southwest Asia, India, and R
ussia in Early Modern English Writing. Stanford, CA: Stanford U
niversity Press.

Ashwell, T. (2000). Pattern of teacher response to student writing in a
multiple draft composition classroom: Is content feedback followed
by form feedback the best method? Journal of Second Language
Writing, 9(3), 227-257.

Atkinson, T. N. (2008). Imitation, intertextuality, and hyperreality in U
S higher education. Semiotica, 2008(169), 27-44.

Bachman, L. (1990). Fundamental considerations in language testing. Ne
w York: Oxford University Press.

Bang, Y. (2004). Step-up learning curriculum, and college English progr
am: A study on students" and teachers" recognition. English Liter
ature and Education, 9(2), 54-63

Barkaoui, K. (2007). Rating scale impact on EFL essay marking: A mix
ed method study. Assessing Writing, 12(2), 86-107.

Barnes, B. D., & Lock, G. (2010). The attributes of effective lecturers of English as a foreign language as perceived by students in a K orean University. *Australian Journal of Teacher Education, 35*(1), 139-152.

Beach, R. (1990). The creative development of meaning: Using autobiog raphical experiences to interpret literature. In Bogdan, D. & Stra w, S. (Eds.), *Beyond communication: Reading comprehension and criticism* (pp. 211-235). Portsmouth, NH: Boyton/Cook.

Beach, R., Appleman, D., & Dorsey, S. (1990). Adolescents' uses of int ertextual links to understand literature. In Beach R. & Hynds, S. (Eds.), *Developing discourse practices in adolescence and adulthood* (pp. 551-553).. Norwood, NJ: Ablex.

Belchamber, R. (2010). CLT re-examined: Some of the constraints and opportunities for communicative language teaching. *Modern Englis h Teacher, 19*(3), 60-64.

Berg, E. (1999). The effects of trained peer response ESL students' revis ion types and writing quality. *Journal of Second Language Writin g, 8*(3), 215-41.

Bhatia, V. (1999). Integrating products, processes, purposes, and particip ants in professional writing. In Candlin, C. & Hyland, K. (Eds.), *Writing: Texts, processes, and practice.* London: Longman.

Biggs, J. (1999). *Teaching for quality learning at university.* Buckingha m: Open University Press.

Bitchener, J., Young, S., & Cameron, D. (2005). The effect of different types of corrective feedback on ESL student writing. *Journal of Se cond Language Writing, 14*(3), 191-205.

Boughey, C. (1997). Learning to write by writing to learn: A group-wo rk approach. *ELT Journal, 51*(2), 126-134.

Boyd, M., & Maloof, V. (2000). How teachers build upon student-prop osal intertextual links to facilitate student talk in the ESL classroo

m. In Hall, J. & Verplaetse, L. (Eds.), The development of secon d and foreign language learning through classroom interaction. N J: Lawrence Erlbaum Associates.

Boyle, O. & Peregoy, S. (1990). Literacy scaffolds: Strategies for first an d second language readers and writers. The Reading Teacher, 44 (3), 194-200.

Breen, M. (1994). Process syllabuses for the language classroom. In Bru mfit, C. (Ed.), General English syllabus design ‐ curriculum and s yllabus design for the general English classroom. Oxford: Oxford University Press.

Brookfield, S. (1995). Becoming a Critically Reflective Teacher: Jossey-B ass Higher and Adult Education Series. San Francisco, CA: Jossey-Bass, Inc.

Brookfield, S. D., & Brookfield, S. (1995). Becoming a critically reflecti ve teacher (Vol. 6). San Francisco: Jossey-Bass.

Brookfield, S. (2000). Transformative learning as ideology critique. In M ezirow, J. (Ed.), Learning as transformation. San Francisco, CA: Jo ssey Bass.

Broukal, M. (2001). Weaving it together 2: Connection reading and wri ting. Boston: Heinle.

Brown, H. (1994). Teaching by principles: An interactive approach to l anguage pedagogy. (2nd ed.). Englewood Cliffs, NJ: Prentice Hall Regents.

Brown, H. (2007). Teaching by principles: An interactive approach to l anguage pedagogy. (3rd ed.). White Plain, NY: Pearson Longman.

Carrell, P. L. (1991). Second language reading: reading ability or langua ge proficiency. Applied Linguistics, 12, 158-179.

Carrell, P. L., & Connor, U. (1991). Reading and writing descriptive an d persuasive texts. The Modern Language Journal, 75, 314-324.

Carson, J., Carrell, P., Silberstein, S., Kroll, B., & Kuehn, P. (1990). R eading- writing relationships in first and second language. TESOL Quarterly, 24(2),245-266.

Carson, J. & Leki, I. (1993). Reading in the composition classroom: Sec ond language perspectives. Boston, MA: Heinle & Heinle.

Carson, J. (2001). Second language writing and second language acquisit ion. In T. Silva & P. Matsuda (Eds.), On Second Language Writi ng. Mahwah, NJ: Lawrence Erlbaum Associates.

Carson, J., & Nelson, G. (1994). Writing groups: Cross-cultural issues. Journal of Second Language Writing, 3(1), 17-30.

Carter, R., & Nash, W. (1990). Seeing through language: a guide to st yles of English writing. Oxford: Basil Blackwell.

Caruso, A. (2011). Error feedback in EFL writing classes: Do feedback t ypes make a difference? Rassegna Italiana Di Linguistica Applicat a, 43(3) 45-68.

Casazza, M. E. (2003). Using a model of direct instruction to teach su mmary writing in a college reading class. In N. A. Stahl & H. Boylan (Eds.), Teaching development-al reading: Historical, theoret ical, and practical background reading (pp. 135-143). Boston, M A: Bedford/St. Martin's.

Caudery, T. (1998). 'Increasing students' awareness of genre through tex t transformation exercises: An old classroom activity revisited. TES L-EJ, 3(3), 1-15.

Celce-Murcia, M., & McIntosh, L. (1991). Teaching English as a second or foreign language (p. 244). Boston, MA: Heinle & Heinle.

Chamblee, C. M. (2003). Bringing Life to reading and writing for at-ris k college students. In N.A. Stahl & H. Boylan (Eds.), Teaching d evelopmental reading: Historical, theoretical, and practical backgro und readings (pp.369-377). Boston, MA: Bedford/St. Martin's.

Chandler, J. (2003). The efficacy of various kinds of error feedback for improvement in the accuracy and fluency of L2 student writing. Journal of Second Language Writing, 12(3), 267-296.

Chen, J. F., Warden, C. A., & Chang, H. T. (2005). Motivators that do not motivate: The case of Chinese EFL learners and the influence of culture on motivation. Tesol Quarterly, 39(4), 609-633.

Chi, F. M. (1995). EFL readers and a focus on intertextuality. Journal of Reading, 38(8), 638-644.

Chi, F. M. (1998). Intertextuality as a constructive reading strategy: Three successful Taiwanese EFL college cases. Studies in English Literature and Linguistics, 24, 49-62.

Chi, F. M. (1999). The writer, the teacher, and the text: examples from Taiwanese EFL college students. Retrieved from http://eric.ed.gov/

Chin, S. (2011). Training Korean EFL teachers to response to student writing. Linguistic of English, 11(3), 68-73

Cho, D. W. (1998). The case of intensive English education program. English Education, 53(2), 113-120

Cho, D. W. (2009). Science journal paper writing in an EFL context: The case of Korea. English for Specific Purposes, 28(4), 230-239.

Cho, H. (2012). Brining models back into the classrooms: Examining the effects of a model-based writing task in an EFL composition class. Linguistics of English, 12(4), 140-151

Cho, J. S. (2002). The research on current status of college general English education and future direction. English Education, 57(2), 365-394.

Cho, K., & Krashen, S. (1994). Acqusition of vocabulray from the Sweet Valley Kinds Series: Adult ESL acqustion. Journal of Reading, 37, 662-667.

Choi, I. C. (2008). The impact of EFL testing on EFL education in Korea. Language Testing, 25(1), 39-62.

Choi, J. (2000). A study on the evaluation of step-up learning curriculu m in English programs. Korea Institute for Curriculum and Evalu ation. Seoul, Korea.

Choi, S. (2007). Is English ability in Korean society a cultural capital? Seoul, Korea: Dangdae.

Choi, S. (2010). A study on writing education focused on proofreading: Examining co-feedback. A Study of National Culture, 35, 301-33 2.

Choi, S., & Jo, I. (2011). Triangulation in needs analysis: For a successf ul journal writing English class in the EFL context. English Lang uage and Literature, 53(2), 231-246.

Choi, S. (2012). Study on the learning method of reading-writing integr ation. Reading Research, 28, 111-141.

Choi, Y. (1995). Transfer of literacy skills from Korean to English. Eng lish Teaching, 50(4), 130-141.

Choi, Y., & Seong, G. (2011). How peer tutoring and peer tutor traini ng influence Korean EFL students' writing. English Language and Literary Education, 17(4), 29-38.

Chuenchaichon, Y. (2011). Impact of intensive reading on the written p erformance of Thai university of EFL writer. In D. S. Giannoni, & C.

Ciarlo (Eds.), Language studies working papers. London: University of R eading.

Cohen, A. D., & Cavalcanti, M. C. (1990). Feedback on compositions: Teacher and student verbal reports. Second language writing: Rese arch insights for the classroom, 42, 155-177.

Collins, J. L. (1998). Strategies for struggling writers. New York: Guildford.

Connor, U. (1996). Contrastive rhetoric: Cross-cultural aspects of second language writing. New York: Cambridge University Press.

Conrad, S. & Goldstein, L. (1999). ESL student revision after teacher-wr itten comments: Text, contexts, and individuals. Journal of Second Language Writing, 8(2), 147-179.

Constantino, R., Lee, S., Cho, K., & Krashen, S. (1997). Free vocabular y reading as a predictor of TOEFL scores. Applied Language Lear ning, 8, 111-118.

Cross, D. (1999). A practical handbook of language teaching. Wilshire, England: Pearson Education.

Cross, J. (2012). Metacognitive instruction for helping less-skilled listener s. ELT Journal, 65(4), 408-416.

Crowhurst, M. (1991). Reading/writing relationships: An intervention stu dy. Canadian Journal of Education, 15(2), 155-172.

Cui, Z. (2010). A comparative analysis of the English writing ability of Chinese and Korean university students (Unpublished master's thes is). Korea University, Seoul.

Cummins, J. (1994). The Acquisition of English as a second language. I n K. Spangenberg-Urbschat & R. Pritchard (Eds.), Kids come in all language: reading instruction for ESL students. Newark, DE: I nternational Reading Association.

Dadze-Arthur, A. (2012). Reflective teaching in further and adult educa tion. Educational Research and Evaluation, 18(8), 803-804.

Day, C. (1993). Reflection: A necessary but not sufficient condition for professional development. British Educational Research Journal, 19 (1), 83-93.

Day, R. R., & Bamford, J. (1998). Extensive reading in the second lan guage classroom. Cambridge: Cambridge University Press.

De Larios, J. R., Murphy, L., & Manchon, R. (1999). The use of restru cturing strategies in EFL writing: A study of Spanish learners of

English as a foreign language. Journal of Second Language Writin g, 8(1), 13-44.

Dewar, B. A., Servos, J. E., Bosacki, S. L., & Coplan. (2013). Early chi ldhood educators' reflections on teaching practices: The role of ge nder and culture. Reflective Practice, 14(3), 381-391.

Dinkelman, T. (2003). Self-study in teacher education a means and end s tool for promoting reflective teaching. Journal of Teacher Educa tion, 54(1), 6-18.

Dornyei, Z. (2001). Teaching and researching motivation. New York: P earson Education.

Dresser, N. (1996). Multicultural manners: New rules of etiquette for a changing society. New York: John Willey & Sons.

Drucker, M. (2003). What reading teachers should know about ESL lea rners. The Reading Teacher, 57(1), 22-29.

Eckhoff, B. (1993). How reading affects children's writing. Language Ar ts, 60(5), 607-616.

Ede, L., & Lunsford, A. (1990). Singular texts/plural authors. Carbondal e, IL: Southern Illinois University Press.

Egan-Robertson, A. (1998). Learning about culture, language, and powe r: Understanding relationships among personhood, literacy practice s, and intertextuality. Journal of Literacy research, 30(4), 449-487.

Elbro, C. & Petersen, D. K. (2004). Long-term effects of phoneme awa reness and letter sound training: An intervention study with child ren at risk for dyslexia. Journal of Educational Psychology, 96(4), 660-670.

Eldred, J. (2002). Moving on with confidence: Perceptions of success in teaching and learning adult literacy. Niace: Leicester.

El-Hindi, A. E. (2003). Connecting reading and writing college learners' metacognitive awareness. In N.A. Stahl & H. Boylan (Eds.), Teach ing developmental reading: Historical, theoretical, and practical bac kground readings (pp. 350-361). Boston, MA: Bedford/St. Martin's.

Elley, W. (1991). Acquiring literacy in a second language: The effect of book based programs. Language Learning, 41(1), 375-411.

Ellis, R. (1994). A study of second language acquisition. Oxford: Oxfor d University Press.

Enginarlar, H. (1993). Student response to teacher feedback in EFL writ ing. System, 21(2), 193-204.

Esmaeili, H. (2002). Integrated reading and writing tasks and ESL stud ents' reading and writing performance in an English language tes t. The Canadian Modern Language Review, 58(4), 599-622.

Falk-Ross, F. C. (2003). Toward the new literacy: changes in college st udents' reading comprehension strategies following reading/writing projects. In N.A. Stahl & H. Boylan (Eds.), Teaching developmen tal reading: Historical, theoretical, and practical background readin gs (pp. 111-125). Boston, MA: Bedford/St. Martin's.

Fathman, K., & Whalley, A. (1990). Teacher response to student writin g: Focus on form versus content. In B. Kroll (Ed.), Second langu age writing: Research insights for the classroom. Cambridge: Cam bridge University Press.

Ferris, D. (1995). Students reaction to teacher response in multiple-draft composition classrooms. TESOL Quarterly, 29(1), 33-53.

Ferris, D. (1999). The case for grammar correction in L2 writing classes: A resp onse to Truscott (1996). Journal of Second Language Writing, 8(1), 1-11.

Ferris, D. (2003). Responding to Writing. In B. Kroll (Ed.), Exploring the dynamics of second language writing. Cambridge: Cambridge University Press.

Ferris, D., & Hedgcock, J. (1998). Teaching ESL composition: Purpose, process, and practice. Mahwah, NJ: Lawrence Erlbaum.

Ferris, D., & Hedgcock, J. (2005). Teaching ESL composition: purpose, process, and practice (2nd ed). Mahwah, NJ: Lawrence Erlbaum.

Ferris, D., & Roberts, B. (2001). Error feedback in L2 writing classes: How explicit does it need to be?. Journal of second language writing, 10(3), 161-184.

Field, Y., & Oi, Y. (1992). A comparison of internal conjunctive cohesion in the English essay writing of Cantonese speakers and native speakers of English. RELC journal, 23(1), 15-28.

Fitzherald J., & Noblit, G. (1999). About hopes, aspirations, and uncertainty: First-grade English-language learners' emergent reading. Journal of Literacy Research, 31(2), 133-182.

Franklin, E. (Ed.). (1999). Reading and writing in more than one language: Lessons for teachers. Alexandria, VA: TESOL.

Franzen, D. (1995). The effects of grammar supplementation on written accuracy in an intermediate Spanish content course. Modern Language Journal, 79(3), 329-344.

Freeman, D. (1992). Language teacher education, emerging discourse, and change in classroom practice. In Flowerdew, J., M. Brock, and S. Hsia (eds.), Perspectives on second language teacher education. Hong Kong: City Polytechnic of Hong Kong.

Gao, X. (2013). Reflexive and reflective thinking: A crucial link between agency and autonomy. Innovation in Language Learning and Teaching, 7(3), 226-237.

Gibson, K. (2010). Through the eyes of the pre-service teacher: Using a reflective reading journey to inform teaching and learning. Issues in Teacher Education, 19(1), 109-120.

Go, J. C. (2012). Teaching as goal-less and reflective design: A conversation with Herbert A. Simon and Donald Schn. Teachers and Teaching, 18(5), 513-524.

Grabe, W. (2000). Notes towards a theory of second language writing. In T. Silva & P. Matsuda (Eds.), On second language writing (p p. 39-58). Mahwah, NJ: Lawrence Erlbaum Associates.

Grabe, W. (2003). Reading and writing relations: Second language pers pectives on research and practice. In B. Kroll (Ed.), Exploring the dynamics of second language writing. Cambridge: Cambridge Univ ersity Press. 242-262

Grabe, W. (2004). Reading and writing relations: Second language pers pectives on research and practice. In B. Kroll (Ed.), Exploring the dynamics of second language writing (pp.230-258). Cambridge: Ca mbridge University Press.

Grabe, W., & Kaplan, R. (1996). Theory and practice of writing. New York: Longman.

Grabe, W., & Kaplan, R. (1998). Theory and practice of writing: An a pplied linguistic perspective. London: Longman.

Green, J., & Meyer, L. (1991). Toward a critical sociology of reading P edagogy. New York: John Benjamins Publishing Company.

Greene, S. (1992). Mining texts in reading to write. Journal of Advance d Composition, 21(1), 151-170.

Greene, S. (1993). The role of task in the development of academic thi nking through reading and writing in a college history course. Re search in the Teaching of English, 27(1), 46-75.

Gui-ying, S. (2006). A Relevance-Theoretic Approach to Intertextuality Renderings. Shandong Foreign Language Teaching Journal, 1(25), 124-130.

Gutierrez, K. (1992). A comparison of instructional contexts in writing process classrooms with Latino children. Education and Urban Soci ety,24, 140-151.

Ha, M. J. & Schallert, D. L. (2011). Working with intertextuality: Doe s it matter to the teaching of English writing? Applied Linguistic s, 27(1), 87-91.

Hagevik, R., Aydeniz, M., & Rowell, C. G. (2012). Using action resear ch in middle level teacher education to evaluate and deepen reflec tive practice. Teaching and Teacher Education, 28(5), 112-123.

Hamp-Lyons, L. (1991). Assessing second language writing in academic contexts. Norwood, NJ: Ablex Publishing Corporation.

Hare, V. C. (1992). Summarizing text. In J. W. Irwin & M. A. Doyle (Eds.), Reading/writing Connections: Learning from research (pp. 9 6-118). Newark, DE: International Reading Association.

Harklau, L. (2002). The role of writing in classroom second language a cquisition. Journal of Second Language Writing, 11(4), 329-350.

Harmer, J. (2001). The practice of language teaching. London: Longman.

Hartman, D. K. (1995). Eight readers reading: The intertextual links of proficient readers reading multiple passages. Reading Research Qua rterly, 30(3), 520-561.

Hatim, B., & Mason, I. (1990). Discourse and the translator. London/N ew York: Longman.

Hatton, N., & Smith, D. (1995). Reflection in teacher education: Towar ds definition and implementation. Teaching and teacher education, 11(1), 33-49.

Hayes, J. R. (1996). A new framework for understanding cognition and affect in writing. In C. M. Levy & S. E. Ransdell (Eds.), The scien ce of writing: Theories, methods, individual differences, and applicati ons (pp. 1-27). Mahwah, New Jersey: Lawrence Erlbaum Associates.

Heaton, J. B. (1998). Writing English language tests. London and New York: Longman.

Hidi, S., & Boscolo, P. (2006). Motivation and writing. In C. A. MacA rthur, S. Graham, & J. Fitzgerald (Eds.), Handbook of writing res earch (pp. 144-157). New York: Guilford Press.

Hirvela, A. (2004). Connecting reading and writing in second language writing instruction. New York: University of Michigan Press.

Hirvela, A., & Du, Q. (2013). "Why am I paraphrasing?": Undergradu ate ESL writers' engagement with source-based writing and readin g. Journal of English for Academic Purposes, 12(2), 111-120.

Holliday, A. (1994). Appropriate methodology and social context. New York: Cambridge University Press.

Holmes, J. (2004). Intertextuality in EAP: An African context. Journal of English for Academic Purpose, 3(1), 73-88.

Huh, M., & Hwang, I. (2011). Actual use of that-clauses in EFL writin g. English Language and Literature, 53(1), 267-290.

Hunt, R. A. (1985). Reading as writing: Meaning-making and sentence combining. In D. A. Daiker, A. Kerek, & M. Morenberg (Eds.), Sentence combining: A rhetorical perspective (pp. 159-174). Carbo ndale: Southern Illinois University Press.

Hwang, E. K. (2013). Analysis of lexical complexity in Korean EFL stu dents' narrative writing, English Subject Education, 12(3), 161-180.

Hwang, I. Y. (2010). The use of subordination in Korean EFL student writing. Applied Linguistics, 26(1), 111-136.

Hyland, F. (1998). The impact of teacher written feedback on individua l writers. Journal of Second Language Writing, 7(3), 255-286.

Hyland, F., & Hyland, K. (2001). Sugaring the pill: Praise and criticis m in written feedback. Journal of Second Language Writing, 10 (3), 185-212.

Hyland, K. (2002). Teaching and researching writing. Harlow: Longman.

Hyland, K. (2003). Second language writing. Cambridge: Cambridge Un iversity Press.

Iida, A. (2008). Poetry writing as expressive pedagogy in an EFL conte xt identifying possible assessment tools for haiku poetry in EFL fr eshman college writing. Assessing Writing, 13(3), 171-179.

Irwin, W. (2004). Against intertextuality. Philosophy and Literature, 28 (2), 227-242.

Jang, J., & Na, K. (2013). The analysis of writing anxiety on EFL perf ormance of Korean learners. A Study of Linguistics,30, 58-65.

Jin, K. (2005). A method of performance evaluation in English departm ent. Seoul, Korea: Hanbit.

Jinlin, H., Zhong, C., & Shuzhen, T. (2013). Strategies of English litera ture reading and writing for chemistry graduate. Guang Dong Ch emical Industry, 40(18), 130-141.

Joh, J. (2000). Using the summarization task as a post-reading activity at college EFL classrooms. English Teaching, 55(3), 193-216.

Johns, A. M. (2005). English for academic purposes: Issues in undergra duate writing and reading. Multilingual Matters, 133, 130-139.

Jones, J. L., & Jones, K. A. (2013). Teaching reflective practice: Imple mentation in the teacher-education setting, The Teacher Educator, 48(1), 73-85.

Jung, D. S., & Kim, H. D. (2001). A study on the change of college EGP classes. English Education, 56(4), 97-105.

Kamimura, T. (2000). Integration of process and product orientations in EFL writing in struction. RELC Journal, 31(2), 1-28.

Kang, H. (2011). The relationship between different dimensions of lexic al proficiency and writing quality of Korean EFL learners. Applied Linguistics, 27(3), 81-104.

Kelly, P. R., & Farnan, N. (1991). Promoting critical thinking reading through response logs: A reader-response approach with fourth gra ders. In P. Zutell & S. McCormick (Eds.), Learner factors/teacher factors: Issues in literacy research and instruction. Fortieth yearboo k of the National Reading Conference (pp. 277-284). Rochester, NY: National Reading Conference.

Kennedy, S. Y., & Smith, J. B. (2013). The relationship between school collective reflective practice and teacher physiological efficacy sourc es. Teaching and Teacher Education, 29(1), 132-143.

Kim, D., Jung, D., Jang, S., & Eum, C. (1999). Developing of the pro per English educational model in industrial colleges. English Educa tion, 54(1), 121-130.

Kim, E. Y. (2011). Using translation exercises in the communicative EF L writing classroom. ELT journal, 65(2), 154-160.

Kim, K. J. (2004). "Global English" implementing and effect: Practice English programs for college students. Foreign Language Education, 11(3), 58-67.

Kim, K. J. (2006). Writing apprehension and writing achievement of K orean EFL college students. English Teaching, 61(1), 135-154.

Kim, S. (2001). Characteristics of EFL readers' summary writing: A stud y with Korean university students. Foreign Language Annals, 34 (6), 569-581.

Kim, S. Y. (2012). A study on the English read-writing integration: An EFL college composition class. Studies in English Education, 17(1), 27-64.

Kim, H., & Krashen, S. (1997). Why don't language acquirers take ad vantage of the power of reading? TESOL Quarterly, 6(3), 26-37.

Kimura, Y. (2001). Language learning motivation of EFL learners in Ja pan: A cross-sectional analysis of various learning milieus. JALT J ournal, 23(1), 47-68.

King, P. M., & Kitchener, K. S. (1994). Developing reflective judgmen t: Understanding and promoting intellectual growth and critical t hinking in adolescents and adults (pp. 124-188). San Francisco: Jo ssey-Bass Publishers.

Kitchakam, O. (2012). Using blogs to improve students' summary writi ng abilities. Journal of Distance Education, 13(4), 209-219.

Klerman, D. (2013). Reading, writing, and questions in advance: Teachi ng english legal history. The American Journal of Legal History, 53(4), 466-469.

Knapp, P., & Watkins, M. (1994). Context-text-grammar: Teaching the genres and grammar of school writing in infants and primary clas srooms. Sydney: Text Productions.

Kobayashi, H., & Rinnert, C. (1996). Factors affecting composition eval uation in an EFL context: Cultural rhetorical pattern and readers' background. Language Learning, 46(3), 397-433.

Krashen, S. (1993). The power of reading. Englewood, CA: Libraries, Unlimited.

Kroll, B. (1993). Teaching writing is teaching reading: Training the ne w teacher of ESL composition. In J. G. Carson & I. Leki (Eds.), Reading in the composition classroom: Second language perspective s (pp. 1-7). Boston, MA: Heinle & Heinle.

Kucan, L., & Beck, I. L. (1997). Thinking aloud and reading comprehe nsion research: Inquiry, instruction, and social interaction. Review of Educational Research, 67(3), 271-299.

Kuit, J. A., Reay, G., & Freeman, R. (2001). Experiences of reflective t eaching. Active learning in higher education, 2(2), 128-142.

Kumaravadivelu, B. (1993). The name of the task of naming: Methodol ogical aspects of task-based pedagogy. In Crookes, G. and S. Gas s (eds.), Tasks in a pedagogical context. Clevedon: Multilingual M atters.

Kumaravadivelu, B. (1994). The postmethod condition: Emerging strategies for second/foreign language teaching. TESOL Quarterly, 28(1), 45-53.

Kuo, T. (2012). Effects of applying STR for group leaning activities on learning performance in synchronous cyber classroom. Computers & Education, 58(1), 600-608.

Kutney, J. P. (2007). Will writing awareness transfer to writing perfor mance? Response to Douglas Downs and Elizabeth Wardle, "Teac hing about writing, right misconceptions." College Composition an d Communication, 45276-279.

Kwon, O. (2002). English education for sufficient experts fostering: The relationsip between English education in college and internation ed ucation in business. A dissertation presented in International Exch ange Symposium.

Lam, R. (2013). Two portfolio systems: EFL students' perspectives of wr iting ability, text improvement, and feedback. Assessing Writing, 18(2), 67-75.

Lambe. J., McNair, V., & Smith, R. (2013). Special educational needs, e-learning and the reflective e-portfolio: Implications for developin g and assessing competence in pre-service education. Journal of E ducation for Teaching, 39(2), 181-196.

Lambert, V. (2008). Twist and shout: Student's book 6. Oxford: Macmillan.

Langer, J. A., & Applebee, A. N. (1987). How writing shapes thinkin g: A study of teaching and learning. Urbana, IL: National Counci l of Teachers of English.

Larsen-Freeman, D. (1991). Research on language teaching methodologie s: A review of the past and an agenda for the future. In De Bo t, K., R. Ginsberg, and C. Kramsch (eds.), Foreign language rese arch in cross-cultural perspective. Amsterdam/Philadelphia: John Be njamins Publishing.

Larsen-Freeman, D. (1998). Learning teaching is a lifelong process. Pers pective, 14(2), 54-63.

Lee, G. & Schallert, D. L. (2008). Meeting in the margins: Effects of t he teacher-student relationship revision processes of EFL college st udents taking acomposition course. Journal of Second Language Writing, 17(3), 165-182.

Lee, H. (2006). A critical consideration on college English: Focus on co mmunicative teaching method and native speakers' classes. Masters Thesis. Catholic University.

Lee, J., & Patten, B. (1995). Making communicative language teaching happen. New York: McGraw-Hill.

Lee, K. (1998). Grammar educatoin ofr developing communicative comp etence. Studies in English Education, 3(2), 124-130.

Lee, K. R., & Oxford, R. (2008). Understanding EFL learners' strategy use and strategy awareness. Asian EFL Journal, 10(1), 120-131.

Lee, S. K. (2007). Effects of textual enhancement and topic familiarity on Korean EFL students' reading comprehension and learning of p assive form. Language learning, 57(1), 87-118.

Lee, Y. (2003). Alignments and detachments in writing pedagogy: interf ace between teachers' practices and students' purposes in two EFL writing courses in Korea (Doctoral dissertation, University of Lanc aster).

Leki, I. (1991). Twenty-five years of contrastive rhetoric: Text analysis a nd writing pedagogies. TESOL Quarterly, 25(1), 123-143.

Leki, I. (1993). Reciprocal themes in ESL reading and writing. In J. G. Carson & I. Leki (Eds.), Reading in the composition classroom: Se cond language perspectives (pp. 9-32). Boston, MA: Heinle & Hei nle.

Leki, I. (2001). Material, educational, and ideological challenges of teach ing EFL writing at the turn of the century. International Journal of English Studies, 1(2), 197-209.

Lenski, S. (1998). Intertextual intentions: Making connections across text s. The Clearing House, 72(2), 74-80.

Lenski, S., & Johns, J. (1997). Patterns in reading-to-write. Reading Res earch Instruction, 37(1), 15-38.

Lenski, S., & Johns, J. (2000). Improving writing: Resources, strategies, and assessments. Dubuque, Iowa: Kendall/Hunt Publishing Compa ny.

Levin, B. & Camp, J. (2005). Reflection as the foundation for e-portfoli os. Retrieved from http://eric.ed.gov/

Lewis, D. (2008). Theory and Intertextuality: Reading Zora Neale Hurst on and Bessie Head. The Journal of South African and American Studies, 9(2), 113-125.

Li, C. C. (2005). A study of collocational error types in ESL/EFL colleg e learners' writing (Unpublished doctoral dissertation). University College, China.

Lim, D. (2006). Step-up learning through group activities (Unpublished master's thesis). Hankuk University of Foreign Studies, Seoul.

Lin, C. & Hui-Chuan, H. (2001). EFL students' perceptions of web-base d reading-writing activities. Proceedings of the international sympo sium of English, 10, 121-130.

Linchstein, S. & Kimel, D. (2013). The best IBT TOEFL actual test (V ol.2). Seoul, Pagoda.

Lingling, L., & Jingjing, G. (2009). The dialogue between epigraphs an d text-on the relationship between epigraphs and text of The Fre nch lieutenant's woman from the perspective of intertextuality. For eign Language Education, 35, 135-141.

Lippi-Green, R. (1997). English with an accent: Language, ideology, and discrimination in the United States. Psychology Press.

Liston, D. P., & Zeichner, K. M. (1990). Reflective teaching and action

research in pre-service teacher education. British Journal of Teache
r Education, 16(3), 235-254.

Long, M. (1991). Focus on form: A design feature in language teaching
methodology. In De Bot, K., R. Ginsberg, and C. Kramsch (Eds
.), Foreign language research in cross-cultural perspective. Amsterd
am/Philadelphia:John Benjamins Publishing.

Lozauskas, D., & Barrell, J. (1992). Reflective Reading. Science Teacher,
59(8), 42-45.

Lynch, T. (1996). Communication in the Language Classroom. Oxford:
Oxford University Press.

Mabei, T. & Swain, M. (2002). Learner awareness of recasts in classroo
m interaction: A case study of an adult EFL student's second lan
guage learning. Language Awareness, 11(1), 43-63.

Macaro, E. (2006). Strategies for language learning and for language us
e: Revising the theoretical framework. Modern Language Journal,
90(3), 320-337.

Maloof, M. (2000). How teachers can build on student-proposed intertex
tual links to facilitate student talk in the ESL classroom. Second
and Foreign Language Learning through Classroom Interaction, 13
9, 120-133.

Manchón, R. (2009). Writing in foreign language contexts: Learning, te
aching, and research. Buffalo: Multilingual Matters.

Manzo, U., & Manzo, A. (2013). The informal reading-thinking invento
ry: Twenty-first-century assessment formats for discovering reading
and writing needs and strengths. Reading and Writing Quarterly,
29(3), 231-251.

Marefat, F. (2007). Multiple Intelligences: Voices from an EFL writing c
lass. Pazhuhesh-e abanha-ye Khareji, 32, 145-162.

Marton, F., Carlsson, M. A., & Halász, L. (1992). Differences in unders tanding and the use of reflective variation in reading. British Jour

nal of Educational Psychology, 62(1), 1-16.

Matsuda, P., & De Pew, K. (2002). Early second language writing: An

introduction. Journal of Second Language Writing, 11(4), 261-26

8.

Matsumura, S., & Hann, G. (2004). Computer anxiety and students' pr

eferred feedback methods in EFL writing. The Modern Language

Journal, 88(3), 403-415.

McCarthey, S., Guo, Y., & Cummins, S. (2005). Understanding changes

in elementary Mandarin students' L1 and L2 writing. Journal of S

econd Language Writing, 14(2) 71-104.

McGuinley, W. (1992). The role of reading and writing while composin

g from sources. Reading Research Quarterly, 27(3), 227-248.

Mendonca, C . & Johnson, K. (1994). Peer review negotiation: A study

activities in ESL writing instruction. TESOL Quarterly, 28, 120-1

33.

Miao, Y. (2006). Teacher feedback or/and peer feedback: A comparative

study in the Chinese EFL writing class. Modern Foreign Language

s, 3, 23-34..

Min, H. T. (2006). The effects of trained peer review on EFL students'

revision types and writing quality. Journal of Second Language W

riting, 15(2), 118-141.

Montelongo, J. A., & Hernandez, A. C. (2007). Reinforcing expository r

eading and writing skills: A more versatile sentence completion ta

sk. The Reading Teacher, 60(6), 538-546.

Morgan, T. E. (2008). Is there an intertext in this text? Literary and i

nterdisciplinary approaches to intertextuality. The American journal

of semiotics, 3(4), 1-40.

Mulcahy-Ernt, P., & Stewart, J. P. (1994). Reading and writing in the integrated language arts. In L. M. Morrow, J. K. Smith, & L. C. Wilkinson (Eds.), Integrated language arts: Controversy to consens us (pp. 105-132). Boston, MA: Allyn & Bacon.

Muncie, J. (2002). Process writing and vocabulary development: Compar ing lexical frequency profiles across drafts. System, 30(2), 225-235.

Mungthaisong, S. (2003). Constructing EFL literacy practices: A qualitati ve investigation in intertextual talk in Thai University language cl asses (Unpublished doctoral dissertation). University of Adelaide, A ustralia.

Murray, G. (2008). Pop culture and learning: Learners' stories informing EFL. Innovation in Language Learning and Teaching, 2(1), 2-17.

Myers, J. (1993). Constructing community and intertextuality in electron ic mail. Paper presented at the meeting of National Reading Conf erence, New York.

Nam, H. C. (2008). A case study of improving English writing skills from r eading journals. Study of Korean Educational Problems, 26(2), 37-58.

Nation, I. (2009). Teaching ESL/EFL reading and writing. New York: Routledge.

Negrettie, R. & Kuteeva, M. (2011). Fostering metacognitive genre awa reness in L2 academic reading and writing: A case study of pre-s ervice English teachers. Journal of Second Language Writing, 20 (2), 74-85.

Negrettie, R. (2012). Metacognition in student academic writing: A lon gitudinal study of metacognitive awareness and its relation to task perception, self-regulation, and evaluation of performance. Written Communication, 29(2), 142-179.

Nelson, G., & Carson, J. (1998). ESL students' perception of effectivene ss in peer response groups. Journal of Second Language Writing, 7(2), 113-131.

Nielsen, A. L. (1994). Writing Between the Lines: race and intertextuali ty. Athens, GA: University of Georgia Press.

Norman, M. & Hylan, T. (2003). The role of confidence in lifelong lea rning. Educational Studies, 29(2/3), 261-273.

Nunan, D. (1999). Second language teaching and learning. Boston, MA: Heinle & Heinle.

Olson, C. B. & Land, R. (2008). Taking a reading/writing intervention for secondary English language learners on the road: Lessons learn ed from the pathway project. Research in Teaching of English, 42 (3), 259-269.

Ortega, L. (2004). L2 writing research in EFL contexts: Some challenges and opportunities for EFL researchers. The Applied Linguistics Ass ociation of Korea Newsletter (Spring), 1-10.

Pae, J. K. (2012). How do Korean EFL students perform in computer-supported collaborate writing? Multimedia Assisted Language Learning, 15(4), 153-174.

Pajares, F. (1994). Inviting self-efficacy: The role of invitations in the d evelopment of confidence and competence in writing. Journal of I nvitational Theory and Practice, 3(1), 5-11.

Pajares, M. F., & Johnson, M. J. (1993). Confidence and competence in writing" The role of self-efficacy, outcome expectancy, and appreh ension. Retrieved from http://eric.ed.gov/

Park, J. E. (1997). The analysis of communicational English education with native-speakers. English Teaching, 52(1), 88-97

Park, J. (2003). An analysis of content-based textbook used in college English programs. Linguistics, 3(2), 120-133.

Park, S. (1993). The direction of English education. Hongik Dissertations, 25.

Park, S. J. (2013). Globalized of Korean universities and Chinese studen ts: Comparative cases of two universities. Korean Culture and Soci ology Study, 46(1), 123-133.

Patthey-Chavez, G., & Ferris, D. (1997). Writing conferences and the w
eaving of multi-voiced texts in college composition. Research in th
e Teaching of English, 31(1), 51-90.

Pedro, J., Abodeeb-Gentile, T., & Courtney, A. (2012). Reflecting on lit
eracy practices: Using reflective strategies in online discussion and
written reflective summaries. Journal of Digital Learning in Teach
er Education, 29(2), 39-47.

Peng, D., & Yuwen, C. (2003). A Systematic Study of Process Approac
h and its Implications for the Teaching Reforms of College Englis
h Writing. Foreign Language Education, 6, 130-144.

Peregoy, S., & Boyle, O. (1991). Second language oral proficiency chara
cteristics of low, intermediate, and high second language readers.
Hispanic Journal of Behavioral Sciences, 13(1), 55-67.

Peregoy, S., & Boyle, O. (2000). English learners reading English: What
we know, what we need to know. Theory in Practice, 39(4), 35-47.

Ping, W., & Wenjie, L. (2001). Discrepancies of the Oriental & Occide
ntal modes of thinking and its effect on college English writing.
Foreign Language World, 5(11), 130-144.

Pollard, A., & Collins, J. (2005). Reflective teaching. London: Continuum.

Pope, R. (2006). Critical reading into creative re-writing: Textual interve
ntion in English studies now. Anglistentag, 2006, 101-110.

Qi, L. (2005). Intertextuality and Foreign Language Teaching. Foreign L
anguages and Their Teaching, 2, 130-144.

Quinn, K. B. (2003). Teaching reading and writing as modes of learnin
g in college: A glance at the past; a view to the future. In N.A.
Stahl & H.Boylan (Eds.), Teaching developmental reading: Historic
al, theoretical, and practical background readings (pp. 331-349). B
oston, MA: Bedford/St. Martin's.

Quitadamo, I. J., & Kurtz, M. J. (2007). Learning to improve: Using writing to increase critical thinking performance in general educati on biology. CBE⁻ Life Sciences Education, 6(2), 140⁻154.

Rao, Z. (2005). Adapting the SILL to suit EFL students in a Chinese co ntext. Hong Kong Journal of Applied Linguistics, 171(179), 52-70.

Reid, J. A. (1996). Writing reading writing reading: Constructing the cl assroom as writing workshop. Idiom, 45, 30-31.

Renshwa, J. (2007). Boost writing 4. Hong Kong: Pearson Longman As ia ELT.

Reppen, R. (2002). A genre-based approach to content writing instructio n. In J. Richards & W. Renandya (Eds.), Metholody in Language Teaching. Cambridge: Cambridge University Press.

Richards, J. (1990). The language teaching matrix. Cambridge: Cambrid ge University Press.

Rifkin. M. (2013). English letters and Indian literacy: Reading, writing, and new England missionary schools. American Literature, 85(2), 230-244.

Ruan, Z. (2014). Metacognitive awareness of EFL student writers in a Chinese ELT context. Language Awareness, 23(1/2), 76-91.

Rudman, N. P. C. (2013). A critical reflection of self in context-first steps towards the professional doctorate. Reflective Practice, 14(2), 183-195.

Ryder, J. (2013). Practice teaching: A reflective approach. ELT Journal, 67(3), 145-166.

Saito, K. (2007) The influences of explicit phonetic instruction on pronu nciation teaching in EFL settings: The case of English vowels and Japanese learners of English. Linguistics Journal, 3(3), 16-40.

Sadler, R. (1998). Formative assessment: Revisiting the territory. Assessm ent in Education: Principles, policy, and practice, 5(1), 77-84.

Sasaki, M. (2000). Toward an empirical model of EFL writing processes: An Exploratory study. Journal of Second Language Writing, 9(3), 259-291.

Sasake, M., & Hirose, K. (1996). Explanatory variables for EFL student s' expository writing. Language Learning, 46(1), 137-168.

Schnack, P. (2001). Partners in reading: A community reading/writing p roject. English Journal, 90(5), 66-78.

Schon, D. (1991). The reflective turn: Case studies in and on education al practice. New York: Teachers College Press.

Semino, E., & Short, M. (2004). Corpus stylistics: Speech, writing and t hought presentation in a corpus of English writing. New York: R outledge.

Shanahan, T. (1990). Reading and writing together: What does it really mean? In T. Shanahan (Ed.), Reading and writing together: New perspectives for the classroom (pp. 1-21). Norwood, MA: Christop her Gordon Publisher, Inc.

Sheen, Y. (2004). Corrective feedback and learner uptake in communicat ive classrooms across instructional settings. Language Teaching Res earch, 8(3), 263-300.

Shin, H. (1993). A study on teaching writing for EFL learners in high school: Examining the effectiveness of guided writing (Unpublished master's thesis). Ewha Womans University, Seoul.

Shintani, N, & Ellis, R. (2013). The comparative effect of direct written corrective feedback and metalinguistic explanation on learners' expl icit and implicit knowledge of the English indefinite article. Journ al of Second Language Writing, 22(3), 286-306.

Shokrpour, N., & Fallahzadeh, M. H. (2007). A survey of the students and interns' EFL writing problems in Shiraz University of Medical Sciences. The Asian EFL Journal Quarterly, 9(1), 147.

Shuart-Faris, N., & Bloome, D. (Eds.). (2004). Uses of intertextuality in classroom and educational research. New York: IAP.

Silva, T. (1990). ESL composition instruction: Developments, issues, and directions. New York: Cambridge University Press.

Simin, S., & Tavangar, M. (2009). Metadiscourse Knowledge and Use i n Iranian EFL Writing. Asian EFL Journal, 11(1), 230-255.

Simon, E. (2011). Advanced EFL learners' beliefs about language learnin g and teaching: A comparison between grammar, pronunciation, a nd vocabulary. English Studies, 92(8), 896-922.

Simpson, J. M. (2006). Feedback on writing changing EFL students' att itudes. TESL Canada Journal, 24(1), 96-112.

Skehan, P. (1998). Task-based instruction. Annual Review of Applied Li nguistics: Foundations of Second Language Teaching, 18, 54-67.

Song, M. J., & Park, Y. Y. (2004). The integrated approach to college EGP education: A study on English program at Seoul National U niversity. English Education, 59(2), 123-134.

Sterponi, L. (2007). Clandestine interactional reading: Intertextuality and double-voicing under the desk. Linguistics and Education, 18(1), 1 -23.

Strauss, S., & Xiang, X. (2006). The writing conference as a locus of e mergent agency. Written Communication, 23(4), 355-396.

Sue, D., & Harrison, J. (2008). Reflective teaching and learning: A gui de to professional issues for beginning secondary teachers. LA, C A: Sage

Sung, K., Pho, K., & Lee, H. (2004). Developing a model of step-up l earning curriculum. Foreign Languages Education, 11(2), 131-145.

Susser, B. (1994). Process approaches in ESL/EFL writing instruction. Jo urnal of Second Language Writing, 3(1), 31-47.

Swain, M. (1993). The output hypothesis: Just speaking and writing are n't enough. The Canadian Modern Language Review, 50(1), 158-1 64.

Swales, J. (1990). Non-native speaker graduate engineering students and their introductions: Global coherence and local management. In U. Connor & A. John (Eds.), Coherence: Research and pedagogica l perspectives. Washington, DC: TESOL.

Swanson, H.L., & Berninger, V. (1996). Individual differences in childre n's Working memory and writing skill. Journal of Experimental C hild Psychology, 63(2), 358-385.

Thomas, R. F. (1999). Reading Virgil and his texts: studies in intertext uality. New York: University of Michigan Press.

Thonus, T. (1993). Tutors as teachers: Assisting ESL/EFL students in th e writing center. Writing Center Journal, 13(2), 13-26.

Tierney R. & Shanahan, T. (1996). Research on the Reading-Writing Re lationship: Interactions, Transactions, and Outcomes. In R. Barr, M. L. Kamil, P. Mosenthal, & P. D. Pearson (Eds.), Handbook o f Reading Research , 2, 246-280. Mahwah, NJ: Lawrence Erlbau m Associates.

Tomcho, T., & Foels, R. (2012). Meta-analysis of group learning activiti es: Empirically based teaching recommendations. Teaching of Psyc hology, 39(3), 159-169.

Tono, Y., & Kanatani, K. (1995). EFL learners' proficiency and roles of feedback: towards the most appropriate feedback for EFL writing. Annual Review of English Language Education in Japan, 6, 1-11.

Tok, S. & Dolapcioglu, S. D. (2013). Reflective teaching practices in T urkish primary school teachers. Teacher Development, 17(2), 265-287.

Tribble, C. (1996). Writing (Language teaching: A scheme for teacher e ducation). Oxford: Oxford University Press.

Truscott, J. (1996). The case against grammar correction in L2 writing classes. Language Learning, 46(2), 327-369.

Truscott, J. (1999). The case for "The case against grammar correction

in L2 writing classes": A response to Ferris. Journal of Second La
nguage Writing, 8(2), 111-122.

Tsang, W. K. (1996). Comparing the effects of reading and writing on
writing performance. Applied Linguistics, 17(2), 210-233.

Valdes, G. (1999). Incipient bilingualism and the development of Englis
h language writing abilities in the secondary school. In C. Faltis
& P. Wolfe (Eds.), So much to say: Adolescents, bilingualism, an
d ESL in the secondary school. New York: Teachers College Pres
s.

Valeri-Gold, M., & Deming, M. P. (2000). Reading, writing, and the c
ollege developmental student. In R. F. Flippo & D. C. Caverly (E
ds.), Handbook of college reading and study research (pp. 149-17
4). Mahwah, NJ: Erlbaum.

Vygotsky, L. (2012). Thought and language. E. Hanfmann, G. Vakar,
& A. Kozulin (Eds.). Cambridge, MA: MIT Press. Wang, S. H.,
& Wang, Q. (2006). A Review of Hatim's Intertextuality-base Tr
anslation Theory. Journal of PLA University of Foreign Languages,
29(1), 60-63.

Warin, J., Maddock, M., Pell, A., & Hargreaves, L. (2006). Resolving i
dentity dissonance through reflective and reflexive practice in teach
ing. Reflective Practice, 7(2), 233-245.

Washbonme, K. (2012). Active, strategic reading for translation trainees:
Foundations for transactional methods. Translation & Interpreting,
4(1), 38-55.

Watts-Taffe, S., & Truscott, D. (2000). Using what we know about lan
guage and literacy development for ESL students in the mainstrea
m classroom. Language Arts, 77(3), 258-265.

Weigle, S. (2002). Assessing writing. Cambridge: Cambridge University Press.

Williams, J. (2005). Teaching writing in second and foreign language cl assrooms. Boston, MA: McGraw-Hill.

Worton, M. (1990). Intertextuality: Theories and practices. Manchester, New York: Manchester University Press.

Xiangyun, D. L. W. (2007). A Study of the Efficacy of Recitation Input for the Development of Chinese Tertiary-level Students' L2 Writing Proficiency. Foreign Language Education, 4 (15), 68-79.

Yan, C. (2004). Implementation of Formative Evaluation in an EFL Writing Course for Chinese College Non-Language Majors. Foreign Language Education, 5, 111-123.

Yang, M., Badger, R., & Yu, Z. (2006). A comparative study of peer and teacher feedback in a Chinese EFL writing class. Journal of Second Language Writing, 15(3), 179-200.

Yeh, S. W. (2001). Effects of learner control and learning strategies on English as a foreign language (EFL) learning from interactive hypermedia lessons. Journal of Educational Multimedia and Hypermedia, 10(2), 141-160.

Yi, J. Y. (2010). The characteristics of Korean EFL college students' peer feedback to English writing and their perception of the peer feedback. Modern English Education, 11(3), 134-161.

Yinger, R. (1990). The conversation of practice. In R. Clift, W. Houston, & M. Pugach (eds.), Encouraging reflective practice in education. New York: Teachers College Press.

Yoo, I. W. H. (2008). Teaching the academic body paragraph in content-based instruction. English Education, 63(3) 119-133.

Yoon, K., & Lee, J. (2014). Effects of writing genre on EFL learners' English writing performance. Research on English Language Teaching, 13(2), 133-152.

Yule, G., & Tarone, E. (1990). Eliciting the performance of strategic competence. In Scarcella, R., Andersen, E., & Krashen, S. (Eds.). D eveloping Communicative Competence in a Second Language. New York: Newbury House.

Zeichner, K. (1994). Research on teacher thinking and different views o f reflective practice in teaching and teacher education. Teachers' minds and actions: Research on teachers' thinking and practice, 4 5, 9-27.

Zeichner, K. & Liston, D. (1996). Reflective teaching: An introduction. Mahwah, NJ: Lawrence Erlbaum Associates.

Zemach, D. (2009). Sentence writing: Student book. Oxford: Macmillan.

Zemach, D., & Lumisek, L. (2003). College writing: From paragraph to essay. Oxford: Macmillan.

Zhang, L. J. (2001). A dynamic metacognitive systems account of Chine se university students' knowledge about EFL reading. TESOL Qua rterly, 44(2), 320-353.

Zhixue, L., & Shaoshan, L. (2003). Reflections on contemporary research on EFL writing in China - A survey of articles published in eight of the major linguistic journals in China in the past decade. Forei gn Language World, 6(9), 141-153.

Appendix A: A Sample of PPT Lecture

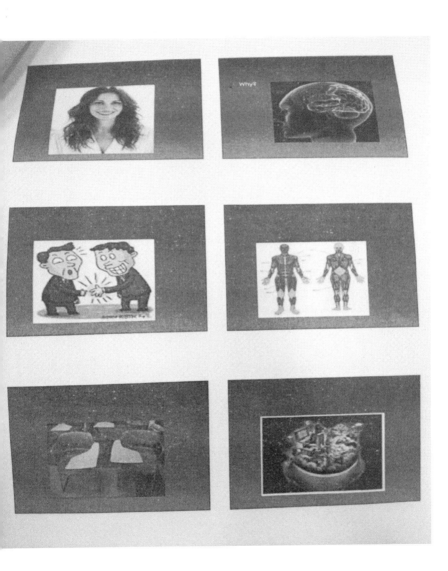

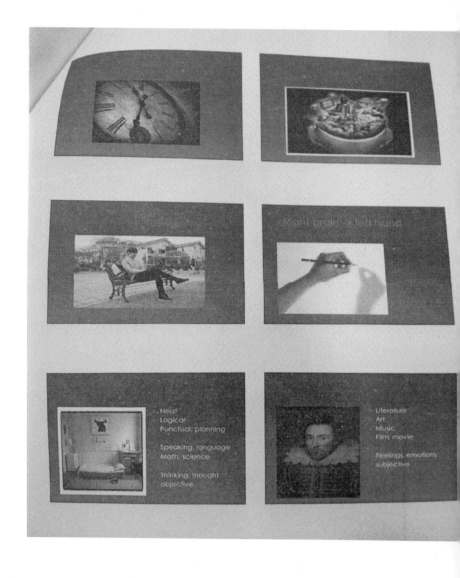

Appendix B: A Sample of Short Answers

1. What do the people mentioned in the textbook have in common?

2. What determines whether people are stronger in the right or left s ide of the brain?

3. How is the brain related to the functions of the human body?

4. What are the characteristics of left-brained people?

5. What are the characteristics of right-brained people?

6. What does the textbook say about both-brained people?

Appendix C: A Sample of Multiple Choice and True-or-False Questions

Multiple Choice

1. People are right-handed or left-handed because of _____
___.

a. the population
b. the way the brain works
c. Paul McCartney and Julia Roberts
d. the messages the brain receives

2. The brain _____

a. has two halves

b. has two left halves

c. is heavier in intelligent people

d. is lighter in intelligent people

3. Each side of the brain _____.

a. likes language and math

b. controls the same things

c. controls different things

d. changes all the time

True of False

1. Fifty percent of the population is left-handed.

2. The weight of the brain does not tell how intelligent you are.

3. A right-handed person may prefer music and art.

4. A person with a strong right brain may be good at recognizing faces.

5. Some people can use both sides of the brain at the same time.

6. A person with a strong right brain may not be practical

Appendix D: Pre-Writing Test

Name: _____

1. Please look at the picture below and explain about the situation in one paragraph (100-120 words).

2. Please read the question below, and write your opinion in one parag raph writing (10sentences).

"There are many ways to find a job: newspaper advertisements, internet job search websites, and personal recommendations. What do you think is the best way to find a job?
Why? Give reasons or examples to support your opinion."

Appendix E: Post-Writing Test

Name: _____

1. Please look at the picture below and explain about the situation in one paragraph (100-120 words).

2. Please read the question below, and write your opinion in one parag raph writing (10 sentences).

"Many companies have always required employees to dress professionally (for stance, in a business suit). Some of these companies now allow thei r employees to me to work once a week in more casual clothing. Is th is a good idea? Why or why t? Give reasons or examples to support y our opinion."

Appendix F: Survey on self-awareness and self-confidence in English writing

Name: _____

I. "While I wrote the paragraph, I paid attention to the following aspects of writing."

	Strongly Disagree	Disagree	Neutral	Agree	Strongly Agree
Content					
Organization					
Grammar					
Vocabulary					
Punctuation					

II. "Are you confident in English writing?"

a. I am very confident

b. I am somewhat confident.

c. I am at average.

d. I am not confident.

e. I am not confident at all.

Appendix G: A Sample from the Textbook

Chapter 2: My Character

"Right Brain, Left Brain"

What do Leonardo da Vinci, Paul McCartney, and Julia Roberts have i n common?They are all left-handed. Today about 15 percent of the po pulation is left-handed. Butwhy are people left-handed? The answer may be in the way the brain works.

Our brain is like a message center. Each second, the brain received mo re than a million messages from our body and knows what to do with them. People think that the weight of the brain weighed 1,375 grams, but less intelligent people may have heavier brains. What is important i s the quality of the brain. The brain has two halves − ther ight brain and the left brain. Each half is about the same size. The right half con trols the left side of the body, and the left half controls the right side of the body. One half is usually stronger than the other. One half of t he brain becomes stronger when you are a child and usually stays the stronger half for the rest of your life.

The left side of the brain controls the right side of the body, so when the left brain is stronger, the right hand will be strong and the person may be right-handed. Thel eft half controls speaking, so a person with a strong left brain may become a good speaker, profession, lawyer, or s alesperson. A person with a strong left brain may have a strong idea o f time and will probably be punctual. The person may be strong in m ath and logic and may like to have things in order. He or she may re member people's names and like to plan things ahead. He or she may be practical and safe. If something happens to the left side of the brai n, the person may have problems speaking and may not know what da y it is. The right side of his or her body will become weak.

When the right side of the brain is stronger, the person will have a st rong left hand and may be left-handed. The person may prefer art, mu sic, and literature. The person may become an artist, a writer, and inve ntor, a film director, or a photographer,T he person may recognize face s, but not remember names. The person may not love numbers or busi ness. The person may like to use his or her feelings, and not look at l ogic and what is practical. It there is an accident to the right side of t he brain, the person may not know where he or she is and may not b e able to do simple hand movements.

This does not mean that all artists are left-handed and all accountants are right- handed. There are many exceptions. Some right-handers have a strong right brain, ands ome left-handers have a strong left brain. Th e best thing would be to use both right and left sides of the brain. T here are people who learn to do two things at the same time. They ca n answer practical questions on the telephone (which uses the left brai n) and at the same time play the piano (which use the right brain), bu t this is not easy to do!

Appendix H: A Sample of Reflective-Reading Strategy 1 (Summarization)

Chapter 1

Name: _____

Please write down one sentence for each paragraph in summarization.

Paragraph 1

Paragraph 2

Paragraph 3

Paragraph 4

Paragraph 5

Appendix I: A Translated Sample of Reflective-Reading Strategy 2 (Reading Journal)
Chapter 1

Name: _____

Please answer the following questions. You may use Korean.

Q1) What do you remember from Chapter 1?

Q2) What have you learned about left brain?

Q3) What have you learned about right brain?

Q4) What you have learned about yourself?

Q5) What would you like to learn more after reading Chapter 1?

Appendix J: Scoring the Writing Tests

Student Name: _____

Pre-Test 1

	5	4	3	2	1	0
Content						
Organization						
Grammar						
Vocabulary						
Punctuation						

Total Score: _____

Pre-Test 2

	5	4	3	2	1	0
Content						
Organization						
Grammar						
Vocabulary						
Punctuation						

Total Score: _____

Post-Test 1

	5	4	3	2	1	0
Content						
Organization						
Grammar						
Vocabulary						
Punctuation						

Total Score: _____

Post-Test 2

	5	4	3	2	1	0
Content						
Organization						
Grammar						
Vocabulary						
Punctuation						

Total Score: _____

Appendix K: Scoring Rubric for the Writing Tests

	Content	Organization	Grammar	Vocabulary	Punctuation
5	Content corresponds to topic and is sufficient to develop topic. *Pre-test: business interview *Post-test: business travel	Link between sentences and paragraphs are natural and united. *follow the sampled outline form *contain all of the three: Introduction, body 1 & 2, conclusion	There are no incomplete sentences. Sentence order and grammar is perfect. *used all of the grammar patterns from the nine chapters correctly	Vocabulary choice and use are perfect. Variable vocabulary is used in appropriate contexts. *used the learnt vocabulary of the ten chapters from the textbook correctly	Spelling and punctuation are perfect. *used the punctuation patterns of the last chapter from the grammar book correctly
4	Content corresponds to topic and is almost sufficient to develop topic.	Link between sentences and paragraphs are relatively natural. Overall unity is good enough.	There are no incomplete sentences. Sentence order are correct and few grammatical errors.	Vocabulary choice and use are appropriate. Relatively, variable vocabulary is used in appropriate contexts.	Few errors in spelling and punctuation.
3	Content corresponds to topic but overall topic development is not sufficient.	Sometimes, unnatural sentences come out and the overall unity is away from the point.	There are a few incomplete sentences. Sentences order errors and grammatical errors.	Sometimes, inappropriate vocabulary is used. Students are inclined to use variable vocabulary.	Some errors in spelling and punctuation.
2	Content does not correspond to	Link between sentences and	There are several incomplete	Several errors in vocabulary use are	Many errors in spelling and

	the topic and it is lack of topic development.	paragraphs are very unnatural. Sentences and paragraphs lack overall unity.	sentences. Sentence order errors and grammatical errors.	found. Vocabulary use if not variable.	punctuation.
1	Content does not correspond to topic and topic development is very insufficient.	Link between sentences and paragraphs are very unnatural. Sentences and paragraphs have no overall unity.	Incomplete sentences. Sentence order errors and grammatical errors often come out.	Vocabulary use errors are often found. Vocabulary use is not variable.	Too many errors in spelling and punctuation marks.
0	Difficult to understand.	Difficult to understand.	Too many errors. Difficult to understand.	Too many errors. Difficult to understand. Not enough to rate.	Not enough to rate.

Appendix L:

A Sample of a Grammar Lecture PPT (Chapter 1)

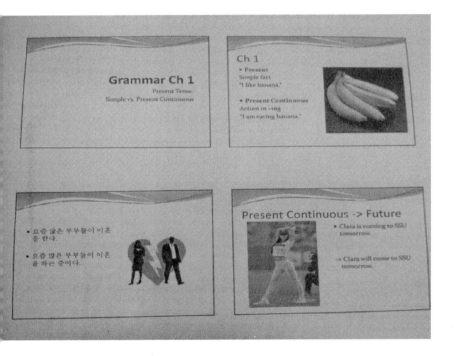

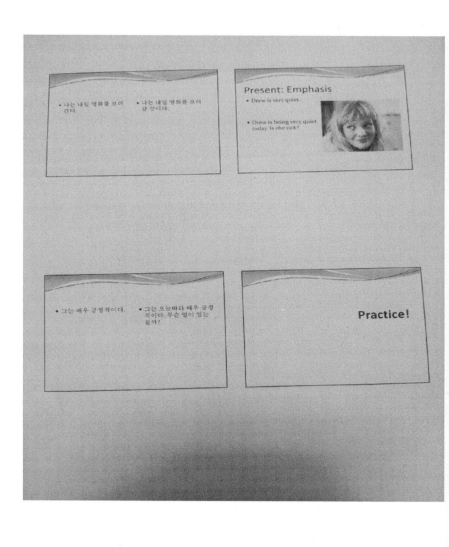

Appendix M:
A Sample of a Grammar Handout (Chapter 1)

Present Tense: Simple vs. Continuous

1. 난 그 반지 살 여유가 없어. 이건 너무 비싸.

2. Susan 과 Tom 이 요즘 사귀고 있어. 주말마다 함께 나가는 걸.

3. Marry 는 내일 Tokyo 에 도착할 예정이다.

4. Terry 의 부모님께서는 그가 회사에서 돌아오는 대로 샌프란시스코 로 떠나신대요.

5. 난 그 사람의 행동을 용납할 수 없어요. 요즘 너무 기분 나쁘게 굴어요.

6. Sally 는 요즘 책임감이 없어요. 그녀와 이야기를 해야겠어요.

| Min-Joo Kim

BA in English Literature at UCLA. MA in TESOL at NYU. Studied in Asian Literature & Culture at Columbia University, NY. PhD in English Education at Korea University. Currently, Assistant Professor at Daegu University.

A Study on Teaching EFL Writing: Reading-Based Writing Instruction

| 초판 1쇄 인쇄일 | 2019년 3월 20일 |
| 초판 1쇄 발행일 | 2019년 3월 30일 |

지은이	김민주
펴낸이	정진이
편집장	김효은
편집/디자인	정구형 우정민 박재원
마케팅	정찬용 이성국
영업관리	한선희 우민지 난춘옥
책임편집	주호
인쇄처	국학인쇄사
펴낸곳	국학자료원 새미(주)

등록일 2005 03 15 제25100−2005−000008호.
경기도 파주시 소라지로 228-2 송촌동 579-4
Tel 442−4623 Fax 6499−3082
www.kookhak.co.kr
kookhak2001@hanmail.net

| ISBN | 979-11-89817-13-8 *93740 |
| 가격 | 21,000원 |

* 저자와의 협의하에 인지는 생략합니다.
　잘못된 책은 구입하신 곳에서 교환하여 드립니다.
　국학자료원 · 새미 · 북치는마을 · LIE는 국학자료원 새미(주)의 브랜드입니다.
* 이 도서의 국립중앙도서관 출판예정도서목록CIP은 서지정보유통지원시스템 홈페이지http://seoji.nl.go.kr와 국가자료공동목록시스템
　http://www.nl.go.kr/kolisnet에서 이용하실 수 있습니다.